CW00394924

VIN ROUGE, FIESTAS ANI

Through the French Canals to Spain

By

Eugenie C Smith

Copyright 2012 Eugenie C Smith

ISBN-13: 978-1480061651
ISBN-10: 1480061654

Published by Eugenie C Smith at CreateSpace

Editing by
Caroline Spence
James Smith

Cover Design by
James Smith

Visit the author website with more details of books by Eugenie C Smith at
http://eugeniecsmithbooks.wordpress.com/

About the Book

Vin Rouge, Fiestas and a Small Boat is a light-hearted, true account of Eugenie and Brian Smith's adventures bound for Spain via the French canals in the 1980's.

Under the murky skies of Essex, England, Brian hatches a plan to build a 33 foot sailing yacht from a kit in the back yard and set out on a trip that would take them across the English Channel, into the beauty of rural France, and finally breaking out into the Mediterranean to extend their adventures west along the coasts of France and Spain.

The intrepid couple pursue their dream whilst juggling the responsibilities of three children, pets, and running a busy overseas property business. Despite their hectic lives, their personable and inquisitive nature leads them on a varied journey full of rich experiences, where they encounter the quirky and often humorous idiosyncrasies of colourful characters they meet along the way. From adorably friendly lock keepers, to boating adventurers, local townsfolk, wayward dreamers, and nudists, they take us on a charming and leisurely drift through heady climates and the intoxicating French and Spanish cultures.

Their endeavours, however, are not bereft of setbacks and challenges. In the Mediterranean, the notorious Gulf of Lion unleashes the wroth of the elements with a near capsize in rough seas. Language barriers, unfathomable local customs, boating mishaps, and all manner of obstacles have to be overcome to continue the journey... to pursue the dream.

A treat for travellers, boating enthusiasts, and armchair adventurers alike, *Vin Rouge, Fiestas and a Small Boat* offers an unassuming, tantalising glimpse of untainted local life and culture.

Chapter 1

We sailed back to England in 1975 on the liner, RMS Windsor Castle, to try to settle in England after spending several years in Nigeria (West Africa), two years in the United States, and five years in South Africa.

We had lived in Torquay, Woking in Surrey, Shrewsbury, and Chepstow during our years in England before venturing abroad. Now we had to live near London so that Brian could reach his work place on a daily basis.

We were finding it difficult for people in England to relate to us - even our relatives; the things we had done and to which we aspired were not much to do with their lives. A chance conversation between Brian and one of his workmates set us off in a direction of which we would never have dreamed. He told him about Newlands Holiday Country Club situated on Canvey Island. It consisted of delightful little chalets fully furnished and close by was a clubhouse and swimming pool. It was ideal for the children who were broken hearted at having to put our mongrel dog, Tor, into quarantine kennels at Chelmsford for six months. We had acquired Tor in Johannesburg and he had already enjoyed two sea voyages back and forth to South Africa. He had done one stint in kennels, which he thoroughly enjoyed as the girls who looked after him spoiled him, and we visited him with a Kit Kat every weekend that he promptly buried in a corner of his run in readiness for a quiet treat should he feel lonely.

Finally, here on Canvey Island, we found people with whom we could relate. There were expats like ourselves who were waiting to return abroad or buy or rent a house to settle in the UK, but best of all the locals on Canvey were down-to-Earth genuine people who took us for what we were, even though we might have appeared to be a bit strange to them. They were the people who had suffered in London during the war years and were used to helping one another.

3

A fairly well known author was renting a chalet near to us who had just published two books - the biographies of Paul Newman and Marilyn Monroe. He had six children, a delightful beautifully spoken refined wife and used to take a taxi to go into London to the Wig and Pen Club and have tea with Lady Churchill. When his royalties came through he treated us all to a day out at the Kursaal in Southend-on-sea... what fun that was and how we were enjoying all these characters we were meeting on Canvey Island.

That was it... we spotted a four bed detached house just across the bank from the holiday chalets, bought it and named it 'Stopover' and have used it for our base ever since whilst we continue to travel.

The children thought it was an excellent choice as they had been swimming in the communal pool at the country club every day and the weather was still warm, so they scrambled over the bank to the pool for the rest of their summer holidays, winning all the swimming races.

We discovered *Parbuckle*, our very first yacht, tucked away in the corner of Essex Marina Yacht Club opposite Burnham-on-Crouch situated on the River Crouch. It was an 18'6" sloop with a bilge keel and ideal for learning to sail as Brian had no sailing experience whatsoever but had read many books. On a wing and a prayer Brian, myself, and our children aged 18, 14, and 10, cast off from the marina one gusty morning to try our skills at sailing, much to the horror of the seasoned yachties lined up on the pontoons. They had warned us not to go out, which didn't do much to boost our confidence as we headed out to sea, unwittingly leaving our 10 year old son on the pontoons – we had not realised he had rushed off with a case of nerves to the toilet. With much manoeuvring, we managed to pull alongside the quay to drag him aboard, fearing we had turned him off sailing for life, but today he is a fine windsurfer and sailor so perhaps it was the only way to learn.

Luckily, Brian's engineering skills came into play and he found his way round the sails and managed to control the outboard *Seagull* engine, which looked much too fragile to get us out of any danger from other craft rushing towards us or heavy squalls blowing up. But *Parbuckle* was a feisty little yacht and rode the waves in a style befitting her. The children and I had the job of putting up the jib and the mainsail, which was difficult on a tossing sea, and not knowing what we were doing. Instructions from the skipper who was manning the engine helped but not enough to stop us from heading towards a Russian tanker unloading wood on the quay. "Stop! Stop!" shouted Sharon our 18 year old as *Parbuckle* seemed hell bent on crashing into the tanker.

"Tack!" Brian commanded from the cockpit and mercifully we all seemed to know what was needed and we avoided a collision.

Green from fright and seasickness, we soldiered on in a fairly rough sea, learning about the hardships of sailing. Brian in the cockpit was enjoying every minute of it with no sign of seasickness in him. That was the time I knew that sailing was going to be a major part of his life, and as a family we would rally round and conquer whatever befell us in our learning experience.

For twelve months we steadfastly braved all weathers and learned 'hands on' how to sail *Parbuckle*, beating up and down the River Crouch despite worried looks from our fellow yachtsmen at Essex Marina who spent a lot of time polishing and cleaning their expensive craft. We joined the yacht club and socialised, noticing the motorboat people tended to keep together at social events with the yachts people hogging their side of the room. Two different animals. A yacht is capable of sailing the world not dependent on engine fuel, whereas a motorboat is limited to how long his fuel will last and has gained the name 'gin palace' as most of the time they are used for entertaining. We found also that there are two types of yachtsmen. Those who dress up in blazers and tell everyone they own a yacht and these are the ones who never leave the port and who have bought their yacht as a status symbol. They try to look down on those dedicated yachtsmen who know their craft inside out and genuinely want to sail the world, learning the skills of sailing day by day. They are the ones whose boats always look busy with all the trappings of the long distance sailor and jobs to do all the time.

During the late 1970's it was becoming fashionable to 'sell up and sail' - a house is a stationery thing incapable of gay transition they said! For some it worked well, but for others it proved to be a disaster as we witnessed during our extensive journey through the French Canals and along the coast of Spain.

As our sailing experience developed, so did our desire to sail to warmer climes. Sailing the River Crouch and the Thames Estuary during the summer was ideal but there was too much time wasted not sailing during the winter months. *Parbuckle*, as much as we loved her, had served her purpose in teaching us to sail and sadly would have to go. An advert in the local paper brought several buyers around and we sold her within a couple of weeks as they could see that she was a seaworthy reliable little craft.

Where to go from here? A family meeting was called with Sharon, Desiree, and James who wholeheartedly voted that we buy a larger yacht. They had their education to finish so there was no question of us joining the 'sell up and sail' brigade, so we looked at prices in all of the yachting magazines and chandleries, but all seemed beyond our pockets. We decided we needed a 33' sloop, which would sleep six and give us comfortable headroom, as our plans were to sail across the English Channel, through the French Canals, and across the Gulf of Lions to the Costa Brava, Spain.

We informed our yachtie friends at Essex Marina Yacht Club that we were on the lookout for a larger craft; they were not surprised after seeing us dashing up and down in *Parbuckle* in all weathers. We looked at several yachts for sale in the marina but none suited our pocket or appealed to us, so feeling disgruntled, we accepted an invitation to go to a party in Leytonstone, East London. Driving through the East End of London in those days was quite frightening but not as frightening as it would be today. We drew up to a row of houses and were greeted at the door by our friend's eleven-year-old son who was dressed in a dazzling white shirt, black trousers, and bow tie. He was the perfect little host, introduced us to everyone there and a variety of drinks, and told us to help ourselves. Brian, in congenial mood, set about trying everything from beer to whisky whilst I stuck to orange juice, knowing we had to drive back to Canvey Island. Needless to say, at the end of the evening he was quite drunk so I got him into the car at midnight and drove home.

The next day, leaving Brian snoring in bed, I wandered over to the yacht club, which is almost opposite our house on Canvey Island, and there it was... a beautiful sleek *Tyler Tufglass* 33' yacht for sale. I knew immediately it was the one we wanted, so I rushed back to the house. "What do you want?" Brian muttered wearily holding his head.

"I've found the yacht of our dreams," I said.

"Where?"

"On the hard in the yacht club... come and have a look."

I don't think he would have dragged himself out of bed for any other reason but he staggered forth and joined me in the short walk across to the Canvey hard, and upon seeing the yacht, agreed it was what we were looking for. The owner was there and showed us the inside of the yacht which he had fitted out himself but not too well as there was no bulkhead between the main cabin and the toilet, which meant anyone visiting the toilet could be seen not only from the main cabin but also from the cockpit. This turned me off and then we were both disappointed to see that the hull had a bulge in it indicating the yacht had been hit by something, but we both agreed that was the type of yacht we wanted and the exact size.

Tylers were advertising do-it-yourself kits. "Brilliant!" said Brian. "Just what we want and affordable to." He fortunately had all the skills to build the yacht himself and we had sufficient garden space in our Canvey home to build it on the lawn. Without hesitation in 1979 he ordered the hull and the deck. It was hauled by crane over our garden fence and he proceeded, with the help of us all, to build the inside and fit it

—

out. Our idea was to fulfill our dream of sailing to Spain and so it was all 'hands on deck'.

Our neighbours rallied round bringing all sorts of odd items, which they thought we might need for our intended journey, and then the great day came in 1980 when our yacht was finished. The grand launch took place at Benfleet Creek, the offshoot from Canvey Island. The big decision of what to name the boat had to be made. Our family meeting unanimously agreed on *Ipi 'n tombia*, meaning 'young African maiden' in honour of our ten years in Africa. We even bought the tape *Ipi tombi* from the musical that was first shown in Cape Town during our years there and then again in London's West End. The launch ceremony was a great success with a bottle of champagne cracked open against the hull of *Ipi* as we fondly call her now.

Together with Bob and Jan, a married couple from down the road, we set sail from Benfleet Creek to our mooring at Essex Marina Yacht Club on the River Crouch. Our adopted crew were both dedicated sailors having built a wooden yacht of their own in their back garden, which seemed to be in vogue in those days. After sailing an 18'6" Caprice sloop, handing a 33' racer cruiser was a challenge, but at least it didn't take off in different directions as quickly as *Parbuckle*. We set off under engine in unfamiliar territory heading towards Southend Pier, which had just recently been badly damaged in a fire. Bob and Jan sat confidently in the cockpit with Brian on the tiller whilst I looked ahead for buoys. "Buoy ahead!" I shouted as we cruised along.

Bob jumped up and said, "Go to the left of the buoy."

"No," replied Brian. "It's to the right." Unfortunately, Bob was a character who thought he was always right and grabbing the tiller steered to the left, which meant we promptly, ran aground.

Not a good start to our journey. Brian from that point took over and Bob became subdued and kept quiet. "Everyone lean on the one side and rock the boat," instructed Brian as a breeze started to blow up making matters worse. We all sat on the one side of the yacht and rocked back and forth until, eventually, it righted itself and we were on our way again.

It felt good to be on a yacht with lots of headroom and space and, as we soon found out, a very fast sailing craft. We set the sails as we headed for Southend Pier and sailed under both jib and main. Bob perked up and was his usual bouncy self again as he too felt the exhilaration of sailing in a good breeze. We put our tape in the music centre and played the musical version of *Ipi tombi* and all felt good with the world.

Passing Shoeburyness and the Maplin Sands, we could hear guns firing as they tested artillery shells and hoped we didn't get in their line of fire. Suddenly out of nowhere, a loud hailer boomed out "White yacht! White yacht! Go to port! Go to port!" Astonished, we looked around us to find descending on us several racing yachts without engines that had no control other than the wind in their sails. We hastily did as we were told in preference to being run down mid-ocean.

Pleased with her sailing performance, Brian guided us into our mooring at Essex Marina Yacht Club on the River Crouch and after tying up and making the warps sound, we all headed to the clubhouse for a much-needed G & T.

Our yachting friends who had known us during our *Parbuckle* sailing days all said they were very relieved to know that we now had a proper ocean-going vessel. They admitted they had secretly worried about us, thinking we'd had plans to cross the Channel in *Parbuckle* who, after all, was just a modest 18′6″. Great celebrations took place in the clubhouse and several members of the yachting fraternity carried out close inspections of Brian's work. It passed muster and we were now very solid members of the club ready to enter races and sail long haul. Little did they know that we were preparing to venture across the English Channel on our way to the Mediterranean at the first opportunity.

Sailing the River Crouch in all weathers gave us the grounding we needed to prepare for the journey. We sailed in thick fog, navigating the various buoys heading towards Pinmill and Ipswich. We crossed the Thames Estuary into the River

Medway amidst squalls and thunder and lightening and I conquered seasickness with the aid of sea bands from *Boots* the Chemists. These marvellous little wrist bands with a button for the pressure point three fingers in on the wrist remarkably gave me the relief from the dreaded sea sickness. All without the aid of seasickness pills which could leave a person drowsy... not a good recipe for a yachtsperson needing their wits about them.

We still had three children to educate, a dog and a parrot we had brought back from Africa with us to look after, and we were both working - Brian as an Engineer and myself at that time fundraising for the charity *Help the Aged*, which took up a great deal of our time. Every spare moment was spent driving to Wallasea Island to the Essex Marina Yacht Club where we moored *Ipi 'n tombia*. We watched with envy whilst our friends from the party at Leytonstone, East London set out with their three children heading for Spain on their 32' wooden yacht. They wrote to us from Alicante in southern Spain where they were anchored in the harbour and told us, we must "do it". They had met a man of sixty years who had sailed to Spain from England, so as we were much younger, we could surely do the same.

Chapter 2

A year had gone by since we had completed the building of *Ipi 'n tombia*. Our dog Tor, who was a stray from our days living and working in Johannesburg, South Africa was now getting old and had lost the use of his legs. Sadly, he passed away, but he had accompanied us on three sea voyages back and forth from Cape Town and been in quarantine twice, which surprisingly he enjoyed as he was very much spoiled by the girls who looked after him during the six month period. He was again spoiled by our three children when he came home each time, so we celebrated Tor's life rather than mourned him, as he had been much loved and much travelled.

Our West African grey parrot named Nelson (since he only had one eye) also lived a happy life. We bought him in the Sahara Desert for ten shillings out of sympathy, and he chatted away merrily on his perch on the terrace in our home in Nigeria - warily eyeing the vultures who circled ahead. He then accompanying us on the ship back to the UK. He had a lucky escape on the sea voyage to England as he was amongst other parrots in a hold with some wild cats that got loose and were trying to get at all the birds. Some of them died of a heart attack but Nelson was made of sterner stuff and lived to sample life in England for a couple of years. He survived a hot English summer with his cage hanging from an apple tree in the orchard of our house in Shrewsbury, but alas died in the winter. This was from eating too many bacon rinds to which he was very partial or pneumonia from the cold - although I must add, he had a very warm spot in the alcove near the fire in the house during the winter months.

We have many happy memories of Nelson, mainly as a mischief-maker. My husband, as part of his job in Nigeria had to go 'upcountry' on one of the old steam trains and I accompanied him from time to time. We had a compartment to ourselves with a kerosene fridge and a steward to prepare our meals. Nelson took pride of place in his smart cage on the seat of the compartment but alas, when the guard blew his whistle at every stop, he did a very good imitation of the whistle and I won't mention the chaos this caused. We eventually told him to be quiet and covered him up with a cloth so that he would think it was night time.

That was not the only time he embarrassed us. When we were coming home from Africa on the boat train, we took him into the compartment on our way to London and he had learned from somewhere how to imitate a wolf whistle. Each time a lady passed up the corridor, he would whistle loudly and Brian received some very nasty looks.

We miss his mischievous ways and feel Nelson was glad we had rescued him from the desert as he, like Tor, had led an interesting life and was much loved by our family.

Our three children - now grown up - were all at university age, so we had the freedom to fulfill our dream to sail *Ipi 'n tombia* to the Mediterranean. We decided it would be more convenient to bring our yacht around to Canvey Island in order to load up for the trip from our house, which was situated just across from the yacht club.

Although Brian was still employed as an Engineer in the UK, he was going to use leave he had stored up to carry out the first leg of the journey across the English Channel. I was still working and busy sorting out the children's education and there was our house at Canvey Island to look after, so Brian decided he would like some company to go across the English Channel - preferably a strong man with some sailing experience. One of the girls I worked with at the time recommended a fellow named David whom I also knew. He had some motorboat experience and was keen to accompany Brian across the Channel and then on to Paris.

Brian was happy with the sailing skills of his newfound friend and the trip from Ramsgate to Calais only took a couple of hours in fairly calm seas. The trip from Calais to Dieppe was, however, quite rough; the mainsail was ripped and had to be taken down, meaning they had to sail under foresail alone and there was no roller reefing facility on the yacht in those days. Feeling exhausted after the journey they took a break. The next day they were pleased to see that the sun was out and the seas were calm in readiness for their trip from Dieppe to Le Havre. Here the mast had to be taken down by a hand-operated crane in readiness for the trip on the Seine. Having heard about the tidal bore phenomenon known as the Mascaret which occurs in the lower Seine almost to Rouen, reaching its magnitude at Caudebec when a wave height of 6m can occur if there is a westerly wind, Brian was prepared for a rough voyage. He had read that the power of the Mascaret was something to be reckoned with as Victor Hugo lost his eldest daughter, Léopoldine, on 4th September 1843. She was drowned in front of Hugo's house at Villequier and her husband also died trying to save her.

The trip along the Seine to Paris, however, mercifully proved to be calm and Brian began to appreciate the beauty of France. Little French children ran along the grassy banks cheering, waving and shouting "Le petit bateau" as they headed toward the famous Eiffel Tower and tied up at a marina in Paris ready for a much-needed glass of cold lager. Then it was all systems go again as they travelled on up the Seine for about half an hour to two islands where they dropped anchor between them. After making the yacht shipshape, Brian and David looked around to see that a couple who were obviously English watching them from one of the islands. They were intrigued by the name of the boat they said and wanted to know what it meant. "It means young African maiden," Brian told them and explained that our family had named the yacht after our ten years of living in Africa. They were fascinated and so Brian invited them aboard and a friendship began.

They introduced themselves as Patricia and John Eccles, originally from London. Their dream had been to live on the island just outside Paris, which they had discovered several years previously. They had scraped enough money together to buy a canal boat and some of the land on the island. Neither of them seemed to have a job and it was quite apparent that

Patricia was several months pregnant, so Brian and David wondered how they were going to realise their dream, as when they were shown the area where the house was to be, there were only a few bricks laid. John said he was an artist and did manage to sell a few paintings now and then, which gave him the opportunity to work on the house. In the meantime, however, they were making do by living on the canal boat that was reasonably roomy for two of them. Brian wondered how on earth they would manage when a newborn baby arrived!

They were a very likeable couple, both spoke fluent French and were extremely helpful to Brian and David – they said they knew the owner of the island who wouldn't mind them mooring the yacht there if they had to return to England. This was good news as David had to return to his job and Brian had to follow shortly afterwards.

Brian asked whom he should pay for the mooring but Patricia and John insisted that there wouldn't be any charge and introduced them to an elderly French man by the name of Christophe who moored his yacht on the island and lived in it permanently. He seemed delighted to have another yacht moored close to him and decided he would look after it but strongly declined Brian's offer of money. The next day, Brian drove David to the airport to return to London, paying his fares and expenses and thanking him for his help during the trip to Paris - he would not be returning as I would be joining Brian eventually to sail through the French Canals and then into the Mediterranean.

Reluctantly Brian had to make safe the mooring and say goodbye to his newfound friends and Christophe to return to work in England. He found it hard to adapt to the old routine after such an exciting trip to Paris, but at the same time felt a great sense of achievement. After all, he had fulfilled part of his dream and was already in Paris, whereas many of his fellow yachtsman had hardly left the marina in England - some afraid to leave harbour!

We were lost without a yacht to sail in England and frequented our old yacht club at Essex Marina Yacht Club but it was not the same without *Ipi 'n tombia.*

Chapter 3

We looked forward to seeing *Ipi 'n tombia* again and when we both had some leave to come we took the opportunity and booked flights to Paris. It was winter and by the time we arrived in France the countryside was shrouded in thick snow; everywhere there was an eerie silence as a lot of traffic had stopped in the vain attempt to plough through the Paris streets.

Patricia and John were excitedly waving to us as we came through the arrivals hall as we had let them know we were coming. They greeted us like long lost friends and Brian introduced me to them - I could see why he had liked them, as they seemed to be very genuine nice people.

"How are you getting along with your house on the Island?" asked Brian.

"Not too well," declared John, and it was apparent that not much work could have been done as it looked as though the baby was now imminent judging by Patricia's huge stomach. "We are still living on our canal boat," he said. He didn't seem at all worried, but they appeared happy together, which was all-important. Brian and I felt that they would work things out and overcome any problems.

When we arrived on the island, we found our French friend Christophe waving from his boat in greeting and seemed delighted to see us. Brian introduced me to him but my French was limited and Christophe's English non-existent, so I realised I would have to brush up on the language very rapidly. He kissed us on both cheeks in welcome, as is the French way, and invited us aboard his yacht for an aperitif. We were glad Patricia and John joined us as they translated for us.

Christophe proudly showed us a black and white photograph he had taken of a whole row of birds lined up on the boom of our yacht and told us he was looking after it very carefully for us.

Brian and I were overwhelmed by the kindness and friendliness surrounding us, which made our first stay in Paris a delight.

We invited Patricia and John together with Christophe to dinner at the lovely riverside restaurant, but Christophe politely refused. He was just happy to see us and enjoyed company as he lived alone on his yacht. We insisted, however, that Patricia and John join us for dinner and we all enjoyed a sumptuous meal of typical French cuisine and fine wine before they motored us over to our yacht in their *Bombard* dinghy.

Christophe had kindly cleared all the snow from the decks and all inside was shipshape. It was great to be back on our beloved *Ipi 'n tombia* again and although it was cold, we lit the little gas fire we had installed and enjoyed several cosy days and nights. We rated ourselves to be very lucky to be able to enjoy Paris in the snow and visited various points of interest. We didn't worry too much that we couldn't sit at the pavement cafes outside because of the cold weather and enjoyed the ambience of the warmth inside instead. It was a very different Paris to the one we would experience on our next trip in the spring of that year.

Our busy lives in England continued, but the thought of *Ipi 'n tombia* waiting for us in Paris kept us going and we planned our trip through the French Canals with the assistance of pilot books and charts of the areas we planned to visit.

Paris in spring is everything it is cracked up to be. We travelled on the Metro system: so different to the London Underground as it was so clean, efficient, and interesting. At the Louvre Metro Station, glass cases contained statues and pictures of the history of the area - all of interest to the foreign traveller who wished to absorb as much of the history of France in the limited time available. How better to catch up whilst waiting for the train?

Spring was in the air and we frequented the pavement cafés - this time sitting out in the sunshine, drinking coffee and watching the smart French women walking by. All around, a bustling sense of excitement as the people of the city went about their daily tasks. The aroma of freshly baked bread pervaded along with brewed coffee. It was very hard indeed to pass by the pâtisserie without choosing a very naughty but nice cream cake, adding inches to my ever-expanding waistline.

Cars, motorbikes, and vans passed through the Arc de Triomphe - a magnificent feat of architecture, every bit as impressive as one had imagined.

The Eiffel Tower, at close quarters was quite awesome, and we were tempted to go to the top to see the view but my head for heights is not good, so we stayed with our feet firmly on the ground and watched others less feint hearted than I ascend its mighty heights.

When we had finished sightseeing, we knew that *Ipi 'n tombia* waited for us gently bobbing up and down on the River Marne, if only we could find our way back to where she was moored! Upon leaving the Eiffel Tower, we wandered in various directions and found ourselves completely lost.

We had no choice but to try to ask a passing French man if he could help us, but communicating was not at all easy as he spoke no English at all. The only nautical words we knew were le bateau. We repeated this about four times until an expression of recognition lit up the Frenchman's face. "Ahh…" he exclaimed,"…le bateau!" And with that, he gestured for us to follow him, which we did, thinking we were heading for the river and our mooring.

We walked quite some distance with him talking away in French and gesticulating with his hands hoping that we could understand him until he stopped outside a pretty little French house with green shutters and white lacy curtains fluttering at the window. He opened the gate leading up the path to the green front door and bid us to go before him. We stood at the door whilst he found his key and he asked us to enter. We did so wondering what was next and wandered through the cool interior until we reached a patio at the back of the house where a French lady and two children were sitting sunning themselves. On our approach, the lady got up to welcome us and I asked hopefully "Do you speak English?" But to no avail, however, we felt we were welcome, and presumed she was the wife of the Frenchman. She ushered us into the kitchen area, which was pristine and cosy. She proceeded to make some coffee and served this to us with some biscuits on a tray. We sadly missed our friends John and Patricia who could have translated for us as we were completely in the dark as to why we were there until our friendly Frenchman then gestured to us to go into yet another room where he proceeded to open drawers and eventually produced a street map of the area. At last light loomed, he was going to guide us to our mooring by showing us where the River was situated on the map.

With a sigh of relief with his help, and much interruption from his wife who seemed to know the area better than her husband did, we managed to locate the river and got a rough idea of where our yacht was moored. With much thanking, kissing on both cheeks, and shaking of hands, we left our saviour and wound our way back to the river and the safe haven of *Ipi 'n tombia*.

Again, we were very impressed with the friendly hospitality and courtesy that was constantly being afforded to us by the French people.

This was our second trip to Paris in the year of 1985 and we were to visit Paris twice more before setting out on our major journey through the canals. We could not believe it was a whole five years since, together with our three children (now grown up), we had built *Ipi 'n tombia* from a hull and a deck in our back garden at Canvey Island and launched it at Benfleet Creek. The trips back and forth to Paris gave us the opportunity to improve our French and gradually we were able to add words to our vocabulary. Because of this were able to get to know and understand the French people better, which would be important if we were to be able to communicate with them during our trip.

We found the Royal Yachting Association booklets were a great help and also the canal/river maps that we obtained in London and Paris. We studied these avidly before setting out on what proved to be one of the most fabulous experiences in our lifetime.

Chapter 4

On 6th July 1985, we set out for Gatwick Airport armed with warps in a suitcase, a pair of oars for our dinghy, and bags packed with swimsuits, shorts, and T-shirts. We stayed the night at Gatwick Manor Hotel and flew *British Caledonian* to Charles de Gaulle Airport. John and Patricia (our faithful English friends from Paris) met us proudly, waiting to show us their bouncing baby boy who had been born in our absence. They said they were still no further on with the building of their dream house on the island due to lack of funds but were perfectly happy to carry on living in their canal boat.

They drove us to the local market, where we chose fruit and vegetables for our journey, and then on to the local tiny supermarket to stock up on tinned food, (*Hero* was the popular brand for yachtsmen in those days). We also stocked up with bottles of water to last us until our first stop along the canal.

We were sad to leave our English friends and dear Christophe, all of whom had been extremely kind to us and wanted nothing in return. Again, we asked Christophe if he would join us for a farewell dinner at the lovely riverside restaurant, but again he declined and wouldn't accept anything at all in return for the care he had taken of our yacht during our absence that year. This was the kind of hospitality we found was offered to us by the kindly French people we encountered on our travels through the canals.

The day of departure dawned with a cloudless blue sky. We sat in the cockpit with the mast spread across the decks lengthwise so that it wouldn't interfere with our movements on deck and we had a clear view from the cockpit. We were fortunate in as much as our cockpit was designed so that we could fit two folding canvas chairs over the cockpit coming and proved very useful as we could steer the tiller with our foot.

The moment for departure had arrived and so we started our Bukh 24 diesel inboard engine (our trusty warhorse), and full of excitement, we set off madly waving to our friends. We spotted a glistening tear in Christophe's eye as we chugged past him through the two islands and continued up the River Marne in the direction of Château-Thierry.

The water was like glass and the sun shone down on us from a clear blue sky. This was Paradise. "Is there any other way of living?" we said to one another. Those pessimists and so called experienced boat people who tried to fill us with fear and trepidation before we set out on this glorious project were very sad people, we decided, who obviously hadn't truly experienced the freedom and spirit of adventure.

We motored slowly down the Marne which, compared to the canals in Britain, were vast and wide enough for the huge commercial barges that passed us from time to time with whole French families aboard cheerily waving to us and calling out "Le petit bateau!"

In front of us loomed our first tunnel. We approached with caution and had no idea whether a barge or any other craft would be approaching from the other direction, as it was very dark. Brian, with his usual astuteness, steered the yacht cautiously through with the assistance of our yacht's navigation lights until we could see a patch of sunlight far away in the distance. I was relieved to see it, as the tunnel felt very eerie and damp. I dreaded the thought of the engine failing and us being stuck in there with a huge commercial barge bearing down on us.

Nevertheless, it was uneventful and we were totally unprepared for the magnificent scenery spread before us. As we exited the tunnel, we gasped in amazement on entering a beautiful glade sheltered by trees casting their shadows on the serene sparkling water. There were no other craft in sight to spoil the magnificence of this wonderland so we cut the engine in order to enjoy the quiet peacefulness and beauty surrounding us. We tied up at the riverside and enjoyed a cool drink and a snack before contemplating carrying on to experience our very first lock.

We wondered how we would cope with the locks as there were going to be many, but Brian had read many books and seemed to know the procedure.

As we approached our first lock, we noticed the lockkeeper's cottage on the bank with a pretty little garden and rows of vegetables all neatly in line. The keeper's wife and two small children had obviously heard our cautious approach and waved us cheerily towards the lock gates. She opened the gates by hand and we motored into the side of the lock. We threw our warps to her and she and the children, who were used to the procedure, tied them round the bollards forward and stern. She then wound the handle to close the lock gates behind us and slowly let the water in until the yacht rose and was on the same level as the lockkeeper's cottage. It was a strange experience holding on to the warps as with the minimum of fuss, the lockkeeper's wife then threw the warps to us forward and aft and we proceeded through the exit lock gates and out on to the canal to carry on cruising down the River Marne.

Although the river was very wide, and we motored towards the centre to look out for any other craft, we could still appreciate the beautiful greenery of the countryside and enjoy watching the antics of cyclists and walkers on the towpaths running either side. We passed under several ornate bridges that gave pedestrians or cyclists access to the pathways; considering there was so much commercial traffic passing up and down the river, it was surprisingly clear and clean.

We motored in blissful silence for about an hour. The time slipped by rapidly until we noticed it was nearly 4pm in the afternoon - time for us to moor up for the evening. We eventually came to a delightful little French village and looked for somewhere on the side of the bank to tie up as there was no official mooring place. There was not a soul in site as we cruised towards the bank and found the ideal spot to tie up. We went in search of food in the village, which consisted of a church, pâtisserie, boucherie, and a garage and so we bought some fresh French bread and some meat for a barbecue. We were to enjoy many barbecues on our yacht along the canals -

23

for safety, we hung it over the stern of the yacht.

We were congratulating ourselves on having found such a peaceful spot. After drinking some French wine and enjoying the delicious barbecue, we decided to retire to our bunks early and be ready to leave next morning. Our peace, however, was shattered when the village church clock started to chime on the hour and every hour right through the night. "Well," we said, "there is no Utopia." But we were as near as we could be to it!

We wondered, when leaving at 10.15am feeling decidedly tired, whether other people cruising the Marne knew about the church clock chiming all night, because we couldn't believe that there was no-one else moored in such an idyllic setting.

We cruised down the river, taking it in turns to sit on the comfortable chairs in the cockpit and controlling the tiller with our feet in order to leave our hands free to drink orange juice to quench our constant thirst - relaxed in the knowledge that we could tackle the forthcoming lock with the assistance of the very helpful keepers. Some of them appreciated us offering them cigarettes. Neither of us smoked but we had been told before setting out for the canals by others who had done it, that this was appreciated.

The sun was becoming unbearably hot and so we rigged up a sunshade in the cockpit, which offered some relief. It was now July and we knew it was the famous Bastille Day on July 14th and we wondered where we would be for the celebrations.

We eventually arrived at the charming sizeable town, Château-Thierry, at 5.30pm after a long day in the sun and thought it was about time we contacted our errant teenagers who were still in the UK and hopefully studying for their exams. Trying to find a public phone, however, was a work of art - mobile phones were barely heard of in the early 1980's and so we were very dependent on public phone boxes. We finally managed to track one down at the back of a small grocery store and the lady proprietor, bustling and jolly, showed us how to operate it and to get through to the UK. All was well and it sounded to us as though our children were glad to have their freedom and the use of our house at Canvey Island whenever they wanted it.

Having put our minds at rest on that score, we sauntered around the town and bought French bread, postcards, and a particularly fine quality of wine for just 50p a bottle from the cave (cellar).

Our mooring was a popular one with a mixture of adventurers like ourselves tied up. They were German, Dutch, American, and British and we rafted up together. There had to be good relations between us all, since we had to clamber over each other's yachts each time we wanted to reach our own. We had found though, that the boating fraternity were a great crowd, always ready to help one another. After all, we all had all the time in the world to relax and enjoy France and its people.

We sat in the cockpit and noticed a number of beautiful white swans floating along the river looking for food. We were disturbed to notice that one was dragging his leg behind him - his feathers were dark instead of pure white like the rest of the swans. Brian thought it might be due to the lead from fishermen's pellets used for fishing. As we were debating this, a man riding his bicycle along the path where our yacht was tied up, stopped to talk to us, we invited him aboard for a drink, and he confirmed that this was the case. His English was good so thankfully we didn't have to struggle too much with our French, which admittedly was improving day by day. He was very interesting as he said he was with English people during the last war and used to drink tea with them in their camps. I practiced some French with him and he appreciated the fact that we were trying to learn his language.

It was 11th July and Bastille day was drawing near and most of our boating acquaintances were looking forward to mooring up to enjoy the festivities. We decided we should look for a nice place to be where we could visit a village that would be celebrating. We visited the bank at Château-Thierry prior to carrying on our journey and were very impressed with the décor and cleanliness inside the bank. We found the service, however, to be very slow which was to be expected we supposed, as the pace of life was very calm compared to our hectic life in Britain.

At 10.30am the next morning, we started out heading for Épernay and by this time we had become quite used to the procedure at the locks for entering and leaving. It was usual to warn the lockkeeper by giving one long prolonged blast on a horn and Brian had a car horn that did the job effectively. In some cases, if other boats were moored up waiting to enter the lock then this wasn't necessary and we would simply join the queue. We found all the lockkeepers very obliging, as it wasn't really part of their duty to attend to mooring ropes. We learned from our experience of the first couple of locks, that if we were alone in a lock without other vessels, to choose to be rather nearer to the back of the lock chamber than towards the front. This avoids the rush of water as the gates open and we could control our yacht easier, especially if the lock was a deep one.

Because of our experience with Christophe in Paris, who never wanted to accept anything from us for looking after our yacht, we were wary about offering money or gifts to the lockkeepers in case it damaged their pride. The offer of cigarettes, however, especially if of a British or American brand, was usually received with pleasure. We found out during our trip that the keepers were very often disabled war veterans - a civil and obliging body of men who were always willing to give advice upon matters concerning the waterways, which was extremely useful to us.

The lockkeepers wife was always willing to supply garden produce at very reasonable cost and we found that they really appreciated it if we offered a pot of jam for her children.

We tried our best to be courteous to the considerate people we were continually encountering everywhere we went. We slowed down to almost a halt each time we witnessed washerwomen washing clothes at the water's edge and we always gave way to commercial vessels who could not manoeuvre their huge barges to the extent we could. We at all times tried to remember that good manners would pay excellent dividends and after all, we were the foreigners.

We pressed on towards Épernay through the most beautiful countryside with the inevitable swans swimming around our yacht. The river was like glass and we could see the reflection of the houses and trees as we looked over the side of the yacht. In the distance, we spotted a church spire and knew that there would be yet another pretty little village not far away. We were right, but we decided to pass by the little village of Juvincourt-et-Damary remembering our experience of the church clock chiming all night.

We realised that we were very lucky indeed to be able to cruise the French Canals in such a leisurely manner. There was none of the abrupt transition of scenery of the over quick journey by train or car. One scene dissolves gradually into another, and only occasionally is this vast panorama of rural France, interrupted by passage through town or city. Woods and forests are the companions of the rivers and canals for a great proportion of their length. Innumerable are the riverside villages in which the pattern of life changes more slowly than would seem possible - villages in which the little local inn will provide you with a meal, perhaps a little roughly served, perfect in its simplicity because every ingredient is local and fresh.

We were learning more of the real France - the France of the hard-working countryman who we found to be friendly, cheerful, and honest. We were now also acquainted with the admirable water-borne families of France on the great barges who gave such heartening activity to the French waterways.

We aimed to be in Épernay at around 5.30pm hoping that we would find a suitable mooring as Épernay is famous for its Champagne and many boating people enjoyed visiting the famous Champagne caves. We were lucky and moored up behind two German motorboats at a small marina and were pleased to see that there was a modest clubhouse of sorts with some facilities including tennis courts. Not that many of the boating fraternity had the energy to participate in a game of tennis!

Chapter 5

We decided we were feeling quite tired and would leave exploring until the next day so cooked a meal aboard the yacht and then retired to our bunks in readiness for the morrow.

Feeling refreshed after a good night's sleep we set out the next morning down the Avenue de Champagne that runs east from the central Place de la République and renowned to be 'the most drinkable street in the world' by Winston Churchill as champagne was one of his most favourite drinks. On either side of the street, there were very impressive eighteenth and nineteenth century mansions and champagne maisons.

We found Moët et Chandon one of the largest and perhaps most famous maison of them all. The cellars have mementos of Napoleon (who was a good friend of Jean-Rémy Moët) and traditionally the bottles are turned by hand - a process of remuage (riddling). We spent an enjoyable time tasting the champagne and went around the cellar on a little train, as it was vast inside and impossible to walk all the way.

Feeling somewhat woozy, we staggered out of the maison and thought we would take a sightseeing tour of Épernay - a very attractive town situated just below vine-covered hills. The town gave a feeling of opulence as we walked along the tree-lined streets and viewed the various small houses open to tour.

Finally, we decided upon a nice restaurant in which to enjoy a leisurely lunch after a very busy morning on land. Restaurants were not cheap, but the food was delightful.

We decided that one day we would return to Épernay and spend more time there as it was a truly beautiful place... not to mention the abundance of Champagne. It was interesting to see the complicated process, particularly the turning by hand, so we wouldn't begrudge in future paying a fair price now that we knew the amount of love and care that went into it.

Back on board the yacht, we set about preparations for the next day as it was nearing the time of the Bastille and we wanted to be in an area where we could get a first hand view of all the celebrations. We set out from Épernay at 10am next morning having to wait a long time at the lock for a huge barge to come through. The lockkeepers were very helpful as were their lovely wives and children. We then motored through an automatic bridge heading towards Tours sur Marne, marvelling once again at the magnificent scenery, and found another idyllic setting... apart from the inevitable village church bell chiming every fifteen minutes. We ate fresh bread, paté, and cool lemonade from our cool box, which we had topped up with ice whilst in Épernay. Miraculously it hadn't melted which indicated that perhaps the weather was a fraction cooler than it had been.

Our next stop was a tiny little village called Sarry. Here we were greeted by two very helpful lockkeepers named Dominic and Frederik who helped us to tie up right opposite their house. They told us that as it was Bastille Day tomorrow we couldn't move on and in the same breath invited us into their charming house to drink Pernod with them. They introduced us to Nous Nous Cleps their dog, and three cats. They also proudly introduced us to their collection of antique guns that they kept in a special cupboard over the fireplace. Just as they were putting them back, there was a knock on the door and the strangest looking man appeared - in fact, he was quite frightening as he was very tall with a scar on his face, unshaven and wearing leather from top to bottom. He looked like a Hells Angel. He was introduced to us as Dominic and Frederik's friend and was extremely polite and friendly. He proudly showed us a medallion round his neck that dated back to 1710 and then to our horror took off his leather top and lifted his vest to show us two horrendous stab wounds. None of this seemed to be in keeping with the quiet gentle man he appeared to be. We went to the door to wave him goodbye with Dominic, as his visit was very short. We expected to see him leaving on a powerful motorbike but to our great amusement, he picked up a small moped from the side of the road that was much too small for him and putt-putted off down the side of the canal, his huge legs sticking out sideways and his knees practically touching the floor as he rounded the corner out of sight.

Sunday 14th July 1985 - Bastille Day. Dominic and Frederik had kindly invited us to see the Bastille celebrations with them in Sarry town. We arranged to knock on their door at 9am so that we could leave early to get a good position, but after we left them the previous day, they must have imbibed more Pernod than they had anticipated, as there was no reply. We decided to sit on the yacht and watch their front door to wait for them to appear. Alas, this did not happen until about noon and they were full of apologies, but without any ado, they backed their ramshackle Fiat car out of the equally ramshackle lean-to at the side of the lockkeeper's cottage and ushered us to sit inside. This was rather difficult as Nous Nous Cleps occupied most of the back seat. We managed to squash in beside him wishing he wasn't such a friendly dog as he smothered us with dribbly kisses every five minutes.

The journey into Sarry was quite an experience with Dominic grinding gears and shouting insults at passing motorists when they got in the way. He was trying to make up for lost time and was speeding down the lanes like a racing driver. We arrived in the centre of the town in record time, but alas, to no avail. The celebrations were over and everyone was winding their way back to their homes for a siesta or a lunchtime treat in the town. It was disappointing, but it was an adventure after all, so we took it on the chin and asked Dominic if he would drop us off at a supermarket so that we could get some provisions for the yacht. As it was Bastille Day, however, most of them were shut, so we made do with some bread and cheese and geared ourselves up for the drive back to our mooring, which thankfully was not as mind blowing as the journey in to town had been.

When we returned to *Ipi 'n tombia*, we found a very nice yacht owned by a Frenchman moored in front of us and we introduced ourselves and told him about our uneventful day.

He too had missed the celebrations, so we invited Dominic, Frederik, and the Frenchman, Pierre, aboard our yacht for drinks. They all said they liked whisky and fortunately, we had some aboard, so at 4pm in the afternoon we all sat in the cockpit and drank whisky to drown our sorrows. Dominic and Frederik seemed to be quite hardened drinkers, whereas we drank very little. Pierre liked the whisky but apparently wasn't used to drinking as much as he became extremely tipsy. Brian had to help him back on to his yacht, not realising that his wife and baby were due to arrive that afternoon as they were all setting out for South America!

She arrived complete with baby, dog, and luggage just as we emerged on deck after our afternoon siesta and was not at all pleased to find her husband who met her in an inebriated state. She spoke very little English but managed to express her displeasure at meeting us as she held us responsible for getting her husband drunk. We tried to make amends - on the canals everyone gets to know everyone and can meet up at different points along the waterways, so it is best to be friendly, as you never know what can happen and when you are likely to need a friend.

We made plans to leave Sarry early the next day to press on to our destination in order to catch our flight from Paris to return to England; we needed to moor our yacht in a good marina and hadn't yet made a choice of which one.

A beautiful Elizabethan yacht pulled up into the mooring and we introduced ourselves to the owners, as the yacht was similar in style to our *Tyler Tufglass*. They were Austrian and their daughter spoke excellent English. They were heading for the Mediterranean.

Finally, Pierre emerged from the cabin of his yacht followed by his wife who was still very grumpy. He told us he had explained to his wife that it wasn't our fault and invited us aboard to see his yacht. It was very impressive, but we were concerned that he had made the forward cabin into a room for the baby, but there was no hatch in case of fire. We thought that this was a serious fault in the design of that particular yacht.

———

Pierre and his wife had already sailed in Italy and the Greek Islands but we were beginning to think it was rather ambitious for them to sail to South America in a 10-metre yacht with a big dog and a baby, but then some people do it and thoroughly enjoy it, so we didn't discourage them in any way. We were playing it by ear and hoping to get to the Mediterranean eventually with trips back to the UK in between times.

Monday 15th July 1985. Next morning at 7.30am, Dominic and Frederick, together with Nous Nous Cleps and their three cats, stood on the quay to wave goodbye and we were surprised to see how upset they were to see us leave. We too were sad to leave them and knew that we would not see them again; they were typical of the French friendly warm people in those days, particularly in the little villages.

Our Austrian friends had left at 6.30am and were motoring just ahead of us - we hoped that we might meet up with them again further along our journey. We had left Pierre and his wife in Sarry (Pierre probably still nursing his hangover, not to mention the wrath of his wife). We hoped to meet up with them again and that Pierre's wife would have forgiven us for getting him drunk.

It seemed as though we had motored through endless tunnels before we finally reached Vitry-le-François, a large town built by François I in1545 as a fortress, that was almost totally destroyed in World War II. It is a significant waterway crossroads with canal access to Paris to the west, Alsace-Lorraine to the east, and the Saône and Rhône rivers to the south.

To our horror, we discovered on our arrival that the bargèes had gone on strike and had blocked the way for pleasure craft. Because of the delay, we had caught up with our Austrian friends on the Elizabethan yacht and Pierre and his wife were not far behind us.

We had to make the decision as to whether to retrace our steps and return to Épernay, where we could leave the yacht for the winter months, and then catch a train to Paris from there, or to moor up at Vitry-le-François staying the night and seeing what happened the next day. We decided to stay and rose early the next morning hoping that the barrier would be up, but there was no movement at all.

We tried speaking with Pierre's wife who was up and about but she still showed signs of hostility, spoke very little English, and Pierre was in bed. So we spoke to our Austrian friends and mutually decided to hang on for a while to see what would happen. It was the right decision because eventually after waiting a day, at 8pm the bargèes opened up the barrier and let us all through. We then went in search of a mooring for the night together with seven Dutch chaps in a huge Dutch barge. Our Austrian friends and Pierre and his wife also came along and finally we tied up underneath a railway bridge just outside Vitry-le-François - a big mistake as it happened as the noise from the trains passing overhead kept us all awake for most of the night.

At 6am, tired and deafened by the noise of the trains, we started our engine and set off once again, heading towards the next lock. I was very grateful to the Dutch chaps from the barge as they helped me with the warps, which meant I didn't have to scrabble up the ladders on the sides of the locks all the time, often encountering rats, which was not very pleasant. Having a large boat, they had the luxury of a fridge and offered us iced drinks for which we were extremely grateful, as we had not had a cold drink in a long time. On our 33' yacht, we could not indulge in the use of a fridge for luxury living. They then cycled off on their bicycles to the nearest little village and came back armed with loaves and yummy French cheese.

To our despair, our next mooring proved even worse than the night under the railway bridge as, unknown to us at the time, we had tied up quite near to an airbase. Mirage fighter aircraft flew overhead all day and night, so needless to say, we didn't stop longer than one night.

We had worked out that with a bit of luck, and providing we didn't encounter any more bargèes going on strike, we could make St Jean de Losne in about five days, which would be an ideal mooring for us to leave our yacht for the winter months.

Still with our newfound Dutch friends, we motored off next morning and our next mooring was so very different to the last two we had suffered. We found ourselves in a delightful setting on the outskirts of Chevillon, a typical rustic French village. When we had secured our warps, we sat in the cockpit and surveyed the beautiful setting in the midst of trees with the sun sparkling on the water and a little dirt track at the side of the mooring leading to who knows where.

By the time we had got the yacht into shape, it was time to look for a restaurant for our evening meal. We wound our way gingerly through the forest of trees and to our surprise and amazement, ahead of us was a tiny restaurant in a clearing through the trees. We had sampled a few restaurants in France but this one was the one that would stay in our minds forever. We walked up the wooden steps to the door wondering what we would find when we entered the restaurant.

It was like a setting from a French musical. Wooden trestle tables were laid out with red check tablecloths. Several men with black berets on their heads were sitting at the tables; they glanced up at us from their game of dominos as we entered the room. We wondered what on earth we were letting ourselves in for, as although everywhere appeared to be spotlessly clean, it did look somewhat primitive.

Our hunger, however, took over, so we sat down at one of the vacant tables. It didn't take long for a waiter to appear, wearing a beret and a red striped apron that stretched round his corpulent middle, and asked us in French what we would like to order. To our astonishment, when he realised we were English, his accent changed to broad Cockney and he informed us he had lived in London for some time and had worked in many of the top restaurants in the city. We couldn't help wondering why he had decided to continue his vocation as a waiter in such a remote spot in France.

We ordered steak with salad for two of us but he returned a moment later with a plate of rather odd-looking cold vegetables, the likes of which we had never seen before. We certainly hadn't ordered them and our thoughts of a beautifully cooked steak with salad were beginning to fade rapidly. We tentatively tried the vegetables whilst the domino players watched us closely with great interest. Whatever they were, they were surprisingly tasty, and satisfied that we were enjoying the French fare, they went back to playing their dominos with much shouting and gesticulating.

We thought the waiter had misheard us and that was all we were going to get, but apparently it was 'starters' as our cockney waiter reappeared to clear our plates and presented us with two delicious looking steaks served with fresh tasty salad. We had noticed from the menu outside the restaurant that the meal would cost us just 12 Francs and so we decided to try the bottle of wine recommended to us by our waiter. It was the most memorable wine we had ever tasted, but even more memorable was the price… it was equivalent to £10 which was a great deal of money for wine in those days (particularly in France where wine was much cheaper than in England). It was, however, such a delightful place; the French men playing dominos tried to befriend us by gesticulating and trying to speak English, whilst I tried out my rusty French.

As we were leaving, our Dutch friends from the barge arrived, and we told them what fabulous food it was, but to look out for the price of the wine before ordering. Feeling somewhat tipsy we headed back to *Ipi 'n tombia*, climbed aboard and were soon fast asleep in readiness for our departure the next day.

Chapter 6

Wednesday 17th July 1985. We decided to set off early at 7.30am the next morning. There was no sign of our Dutch friends so we concluded that they must have sampled the expensive wine and were suffering from hangovers.

I missed their help in climbing up the ladders for me, so Brian took over and he climbed up the ladders on the walls at the side of the locks that were encrusted with green moss with the occasional rat popping his head out. When arriving at the first lock we were greeted by a very annoyed keeper who was expecting the Dutch Barge to enter the lock at the same time as ourselves and but hadn't been informed that we were travelling separately. With much puffing and moaning, however, he proceeded to let us through and we found that, as we journeyed on through the canal, the other lockkeepers had also expected us to be travelling with the Dutch barge but they were not so cross as the first.

Brian cheered up considerably when, at the close of the day, we turned up at a lock operated by two extremely attractive girls in their early twenties - we concluded they must have taken over from their parents as they were dressed as though they were about to go out for an evening in Paris. We noted the name of the village was Brethenay but we had no time to explore as we had arrived late and were ready to leave early the next morning.

Thursday 18th July 1985. We rose early and prepared the yacht for departure at 8am. We arrived at the first lock very quickly where a very pleasant elderly lady with a dog and two cats was waiting for us. She was extremely helpful and friendly which was usual for most of the keepers in the 1980's. We noticed that the keeper's house she lived in with her pets dated back to 1881 and, like many other lockkeepers, there was a large amount of logs all stacked very neatly in the tiny front garden - firewood for the winter months. We also noticed that all the lockkeepers' gardens were beautifully maintained. They took pride in their vegetable gardens, offering us fresh vegetables - in many cases and not wishing to charge anything for them.

We passed Pierre and his wife (still looking grumpy) at the French town of Chaumont, the capital of Haute-Marne, a medieval town with castle ruins and a magnificent viaduct. We then had to proceed through a number of small locks, but found that at some of them, there was no one in attendance. Brian had to go to raise the lockkeepers whilst I held on to the bank with the boat hook.

The worst case of all was when we were near a road bridge and the young boy who was obviously in charge of the lock was leaning over the bridge and seemed impervious to our desperate cries and toots on our horn. Eventually, a passing motorist kindly stopped having noticed our flailing arms, and roused the boy from his reverie into action to help us through the lock.

It was very pleasurable to be motoring through the beautiful countryside with trees and fields on either side, swans swimming beside our yacht, and the hot sun blazing down from a clear blue sky.

Our next stop was at a little village named Hume. As we tied up, a Dutchman who was with his wife and two boys in a motorboat came over to speak to us. He said he had been in Calpe, Southern Spain, for two years but had been fed up and was taking his boat to Brighton, England. He was he was going to sell Spanish property part time, which we thought was a bit risky! Having been in the business myself for many years and knowing how difficult it was full time, never mind part time, I felt quite sorry for him as he obviously didn't know the pitfalls. I didn't say anything to discourage him, however, and just hope things worked out for him when he finally arrived in England.

We enjoyed meeting different characters from various parts of the world, which was one of the many delightful pleasures of yachting and moving from place to place.

Our mooring was very pleasant, so we decided to have a barbecue and went in search of a boucherie and pâtisserie to purchase steaks and bread. A visit to the cave also resulted in a bottle of fine French wine.

Friday 19th July 1985. We arose at 8.30am ready to tackle the longest and most difficult tunnel in France, which is 5km long between the Marne and the Saône. Pierre and his wife, who we discovered was named Nicole, waved to us as they passed by on the way to the tunnel. We ate a hasty breakfast and set out at 9.30am in a fine misty rain. The canal was very narrow and Brian only just managed to squeeze past a barge going into the dock, but we pressed on and headed for the tunnel mouth, passing Pierre and Nicole who had tied up along the route.

When we eventually reached the entrance to the tunnel, there was no indication of what we had to do. We thought it meant that we couldn't start until 2pm, but Pierre and Nicole turned up at 12 noon and said they thought we should go ahead. We went ahead of them because we had a powerful light and a horn, as it was pitch black inside the tunnel with no lighting at all. It was very scary being so enclosed and not being able to see the exit to the tunnel. Fortunately, we didn't pass any large barges on our journey through, but Pierre ran in to the side of the tunnel wall a few times as he was relying on navigating his way through from the light we had on our yacht. Finally, we were all very glad indeed to see the exit to the tunnel after a really nerve racking journey in pitch-black darkness. We relied purely on the light Brian had fortuitously thought to add to our list of essentials for our journey through the French Canals.

As we emerged from the tunnel, we were surprised to find that the weather had changed and it was quite chilly, so we wrapped ourselves in jumpers and got ready to face a series of seven locks going downhill. Since they were in quite close proximity to one another, it proved to be hard work. When we reached the third lock, the keeper told us there was a blockage en route. Hoping it didn't cause delays like the last blockage we had experienced, we pressed on towards our next lock situated on the outskirts of the small village of Dommartin.

For the first time on our trip through the canals, we encountered a woman lockkeeper who was miserable. The keepers' wives we had come across previously had all been cheerful souls, seemingly without any worries or cares. We found later, however, that she was not the only unfriendly lockkeeper, probably because we were now encountering a large bulk of commercial traffic and all the bargèes were finding it hard to get work, hence the strike earlier in the week.

The local people though, were still just as friendly as we were to find out when we tied up along a grassy bank in a quiet and peaceful setting. An elderly man, who was tending his garden in a nearby pretty cottage, spotted us tying up and came over to speak to us, asking if we spoke German, which we didn't. We did, however, manage to communicate in our halting French. Later, when we were settled down and after a meal, he came over to introduce us to his eight-month-old grandchild, telling us that the child's mother spoke fluent English - a fact of which he was immensely proud. Whilst we were speaking to him, one of the authorities from the canal came along to tell us there was a blockage of about 7km down the canal and that we couldn't travel until midday on Monday. We were rather concerned, as this cut our time down again - we had still hoped to make it in time to reach Saint-Jean-de-Losne before our flight to England from Paris the following Saturday.

The weather had been unsettled with clouds and rain, but towards the evening, the sun came out and we decided to have a barbecue. Cooking our barbecue over the back of the pushpit and drinking a bottle of delicious wine, we decided we were in paradise, even though not everything always went to plan and there were hold ups from time to time on the journey.

Feeling very relaxed, we retired to our bunks at 10pm only to be woken by the sound of scurrying sounds on the deck. We assumed it must be rats or field mice as we were moored in a grassy bank area with fields close by. As it was pitch black, there was not much we could do about it, so we closed the forward hatch and kept all the lights on all night.

Next morning it was still cloudy and the barometer had moved forward to a better setting just a fraction. We decided that if any barges or other craft moved towards the blockage, we would follow. But it was now 10am and nothing had stirred on the water, so we assumed that the workmen would be working on the problem until Monday lunchtime and that the lockkeepers would not be working until then. We were still hoping that we would reach Saint-Jean-de-Losne on time if we could get moving on Monday.

We planned to scrub the decks and visit the little village of Dommartin to take up the time until we were eventually allowed to move on. Leaving the yacht shipshape, we climbed ashore and headed in the direction of a little cluster of houses we could see in the distance beyond the fields. The sun was shining by now - breaks in the clouds revealed a clear blue sky - so dressed in T-shirts and shorts with backpacks at the ready for shopping, we stepped out with enthusiasm to see what culinary delights we could purchase.

When we eventually reached the village, however, there was absolutely nothing there in the way of shops or facilities - just a sleepy little hamlet consisting of very old farm buildings converted into houses. We didn't come across any people at all - just a couple of hens and ducks wandering about and two children playing. We did eventually find a doubtful-looking telephone kiosk and were very surprised to be able to get through to our children in England who were obviously enjoying their freedom.

Feeling rather let down at the prospect of having to scrape together what food we had left on the yacht, we meandered back to the mooring with empty haversacks, realising it was going to be important that we move on soon, otherwise we would be without supplies and, particularly, fresh water.

The thought of another night with possibly rats (the worst scenario) or rather less worrying, field mice, scurrying around on the decks above us galvanised Brian into making some rat repellents out of cardboard and placing them around the warps tying us to the bank to stop mice or rats climbing up them. He had read in a yachting magazine some time ago about a sailor who had travelled the French Canals doing the same thing.

Later that afternoon, the nice man who had met us last night came again to see us, this time armed with lettuces and radishes from his garden. We thanked him profusely, as we had no fresh salad aboard, and with some cheese we had, it would make us another meal until we found a village with supplies. Later, his daughter came to show her little boy our yacht and, as she spoke some English, we took the opportunity to thank her and her father for their kindness and friendliness. We really enjoyed meeting the many people who, without exception, always greeted us with friendliness and much curiosity.

As we were sitting in the cockpit watching the sun go down, we noticed that a man and his wife who had arrived at 10am that morning in a car and had parked on the towpath beside the field were still sitting on the side of the bank fishing. They had patiently sat there all day and when they spotted us sitting in the cockpit, they came over and showed us their fish, which were miniscule, but they were very proud of them. It didn't bother them at all that the fish they had so patiently caught were so tiny and were swimming around in a jam jar.

We concluded that day that all people who lived in the countryside were so relaxed and happy with the very simple things in life, that they really had it right, away from the stress and strains of modern life.

Sunday 21st July 1985. We spent the day cleaning and tidying the yacht in preparation (and hope) of departing early the next morning. We took it easy all day and out of curiosity decided to take another look at the village to see whether there would be any signs of life on a Sunday - people going to church perhaps?

When we reached the village, however, there was not a soul in sight, not even the hens, ducks, or children. The stillness was quite eerie. It was as though no one had lived there for hundreds of years. It was virtually a ghost town - or ghost village in this case. We had our camera with us, so took some pictures of this typical French village - we wanted to remember the tranquility and peacefulness we had experienced during our walks there.

When we arrived back, we noticed several families were standing looking at our yacht. It seemed we were the tourist attraction for passing motorists who were exclaiming to one another: "Le petit bateau" (the small boat). Amid much shaking of hands and friendly greetings, we climbed aboard and were offered drinks, sweets, and anything they were carrying in their bags or pockets. We realised that they thought we could be hungry as we couldn't buy provisions in the village and were trying to make it up to us.

When they finally departed after much gesticulating and laughter, we noticed we had run out of fresh water completely, which is disastrous on a yacht journey. We reminded ourselves that we must ask our friend who had brought the vegetables, or his daughter, if they could oblige us with some water to help us on our way as they had promised to come and see us that evening to say goodbye. As promised, they arrived, and at our request, they came back with huge bottles of fresh water that would last us a long time. Without the friendliness and generosity of these country people, our journey could have been stressful, but instead it was entirely relaxing and enjoyable.

That evening, the couple who had shown us their fish the night before were sitting on the bank fishing once more. They came to show us their latest catch, which was not dissimilar, but again, they were very proud. Amidst all this activity, Pierre and Nicole with their baby and huge dog were heading towards us along the towpath from where they had tied up further along the bank. This time, Nicole greeted us in a friendly manner having got over her annoyance with us for getting her husband inebriated - or so she had thought. She accepted a beer from us and said in halting English that they had been grateful to us for guiding them through the very long tunnel. We were glad that she didn't think of us as weird English people anymore and we sealed our friendship with a few drinks. They told us that permission had been given for us to leave at 7am next morning as the blockage had been cleared.

Monday 22nd July 1985. We ate a hasty breakfast before setting off at 6.45am passing Pierre and Nicole who then tagged on behind us as we went through the first few locks together. We noticed the keepers took a great deal of pride in their houses and one lockkeeper had painted his house and surroundings in black and silver which was quite startling, but at the same time impressive.

Another observation we made was that all the lockkeepers in this particular area seemed to keep quite ferocious dogs, which left us wondering whether it was a necessity to own such big ferocious dogs or was it because it was just a popular breed. We remembered our lockkeeper friends, Dominic and Frederik from Sarry, whose dog, Nous Nous Cleps was a very gentle labrador; perhaps it was just some parts of France where the more ferocious dogs were popular.

The weather was surprisingly cold and we were dressed in jeans and sweaters even though it was now 9.45am and the sun was starting to break through. We were noticing the many keepers houses we were passing and some of them were locked up with the keepers living in the nearby village and just appearing when craft were due to pass their particular lock. The houses that remained were beautifully cared for with an abundance of flowers and selection of vegetables in each garden.

Our next stop was at a lovely little holiday area of Pontailler-sur-Saône. It was 7pm in the evening when we arrived; we noticed there were several motorboats and an English yacht moored against the quay. The weather was much warmer by now and children from a nearby camping site were swimming in the water. Some German people in a very large motorboat kindly moved so that we could squeeze in next to them. Pierre and Nicole with baby and dog were not far behind us, so tied alongside for the night.

We all went ashore to look for a restaurant, but because it was a holiday area, we found that the only decent restaurant charged 79 Francs, without wine, which was very expensive in comparison to restaurants we had encountered so far on our travels. As we were on a tight budget, we decided instead to purchase what we thought were Cornish pasties and return to the yacht and cook a pan of chips to accompany them, but when we got back, we discovered they were not Cornish pasties but apple turnovers.

Used to making do with all sorts of different meals on the yacht we enjoyed the chips followed by the most tasty apple turnovers we had ever eaten before and set off for a stroll along the towpath. We were invited aboard a yacht owned by an English couple from Sussex who were living on it permanently and had done some very extensive cruising. Their yacht was 33' in length, which was the same size as *Ipi 'n tombia* so we had a lot in common to talk about and discussed the possibility of joining the ARC (The Atlantic Rally for Cruisers) in November. This was a rally taking place every year with approximately 200 yachts setting sail from the Canary Islands and heading for St Lucia in the Caribbean.

Tuesday 23rd July 1985. We slept soundly that night and woke up refreshed and ready to say our final farewells to Pierre and Nicole who were heading off early on their way to the Mediterranean in readiness for their major trip to South America. Despite our first hiccup with Nicole, we had become quite friendly with them and sorry to see them go as they had been with us for a lot of our journey through the canals. We wished them well and good luck on their long voyage.

It was our turn to leave at 10am on the final leg of our journey to Saint-Jean-de-Losne. The English couple we had met the night before said they thought it would be a very good place for us to leave our yacht to return to England, but could be expensive.

The trip to Saint-Jean-de-Losne took only an hour through the most beautiful river area with children swimming and motorboats and yachts nestling against the riverbanks.

Little children ran along the riverbank and the sounds of "Le petit bateau" rang in our ears as our trusty Bukh diesel engine pounded on its way towards our final destination in 1985.

Saint-Jean-de-Losne proved to be an important junction where boats from the Marne route, as well as boats emerging from the Canal du Rhône au Rhin, converged. We noticed a marked contrast in our surroundings after coming through the first of the Saône's massive locks. The channel widened from a modest 12-15 metres in the Petit Saône to a minimum of 40 metres, and at times, the river was 200 metres across from one bank to the other. We avoided numerous shoals, shallows, and man-made submerged training walls navigating by the red and green channel buoys which were much in evidence.

When we finally reached our destination, we were thrilled to see that the 'Captain Joe Boatyard' was not just a boatyard, but also a delightful marina where yachts and motorboats from all over the world were tied alongside one another. We tied up alongside the quay and went in search of the Mariner's office; we discovered that the owners lived in a big barge with a very comprehensive chandlery next door. It stocked everything the yachtsman could possibly need. We were very relieved to see that they also offered management services, meaning we could leave our yacht in safe hands whilst we returned to England.

I practiced my French on the young French girl in reception and managed to convey to her that we wished to moor our yacht there for a year which she informed us would cost £450. We thought this very reasonable considering the services offered and the beauty of the place so we booked our mooring until July 1986.

Afterwards we discovered the showers, as it was extremely hot, and then went in search of supplies in the nearby town of Saint-Jean-de-Losne. We purchased bread, cheese, wine, and two enormous pots of ice-cold yoghurt and sat in the cockpit consuming this gorgeous meal in the sunshine, looking forward to three more days of bliss before getting ready to return to work in England.

What a wonderful trip it had been and a whole year seemed like a lifetime before we could return to France and to another adventure.

Chapter 7

Wednesday 3rd July 1986. We kept *Ipi 'n tombia* moored at Saint-Jean-de-Losne for a year although we did visit twice by car, enjoying the countryside of France on the way to the Marina. We took this opportunity to transport new sails and other equipment to the yacht, and enjoyed visiting the many restaurants in Saint-Jean-de-Losne. Our favourite restaurant, *La Navigation*, was situated across the bridge where flags of different countries were displayed over the Saône. In the 1980's, it was just a small house with the front room converted into a restaurant. There we enjoyed the most delicious trout we had ever tasted and can remember it to this day as, although we have eaten trout in many restaurants since, it has never quite come up to that standard.

We frequented the local cave, regularly purchasing three bottles of very fine wine for the equivalent of 50p per bottle.

We enjoyed those brief visits to check on the yacht but were looking forward to our holidays in July 1986.

Full of excitement, we flew to Montpellier and then headed for Saint-Jean-de-Losne, ready to move on towards the Mediterranean. We thanked the proprietors of 'Captain Joe' and at 11am that morning took on board 134 Franks worth of diesel in readiness for our journey.

By co-incidence, we met an English couple from a boat named *Water Lily* from Leigh-on-sea not far from where we lived at Canvey Island. They were heading in the same direction as us, towards Lyon. They followed us until our first stop at Chalon-sur-Saône where we had our regulator replaced at a cost of 600 Francs. Much of the countryside was rich meadowland dotted with ancient farmhouses with their distinctive red tiled roofs typical of the south of France. Although it had become a large industrial town and business centre, Chalon-sur-Saône river port had a good upbeat feel to it.

We passed many historic timbered houses, and we were interested in looking around the town as we had heard it had quite a history. Chalon was a bishopric from the 4th Century right up to the French Revolution, and in the 6th Century was the residence of the Burgundian Kings as they then were. We tied up, went in search of the Gothic cathedral and cloister, and came across the Musée Denon, which housed 17th - 19th Century paintings and local folk culture. The ground floor was most impressive, displaying local archaeological collections including a set of magnificent 18,000-year-old flint tools from nearby Volgu.

After a day of exploration, we found our way back to the yacht and were deciding where to dine that evening, when we heard someone banging on the foredeck. An American chap from a huge motorboat moored next to us asked us if we would like to go aboard for a drink.

Although we were whacked out, we felt it would be impolite not to do so, so we thanked him for the offer and climbed aboard their very spacious luxurious motorboat which made our 33 ' yacht seem tiny in comparison. We found all Americans we met on our journey were very hospitable and friendly. They pressed whisky on Brian and although I tried to make my gin and tonic last out, I couldn't get away with less than three before we finally left them telling them we were going in search of a restaurant.

We had no idea where we would find a restaurant, and in a somewhat hazy state of mind, we climbed onto the pontoons and made our way across a rather shaky little bridge heading in the direction of Chalon-sur-Saône. We wound our way round tiny streets and eventually came upon a very charming French bar and restaurant. It resembled a small English pub inasmuch as small tables were dotted around a cosy room with flowers on each table. We seated ourselves and immediately a waiter appeared with the menu. There the resemblance to an English pub ended, as our French was not good at the best of times, and now that we were somewhat inebriated, it was even worse. We couldn't understand any of the items on the menu.

We decided, however, on a main dish of what we thought would be pork chops, but were horrified to see when the waiter returned, that we had ordered pig's trotters swilling around in some unknown liquid. Up until that point, the food we had enjoyed at all the restaurants along the French Canals had been excellent, but we had no idea how to go about tackling the pig's trotters. Each time we poked them with our fork, they bounced back, so we ended up eating nothing and finally ordered a salad in desperation - at least we knew how to ask for that in French. Unwisely, we had wine with the meal, so feeling very tipsy, we eventually staggered back to the pontoons, marginally avoiding falling into the water and at the same time trying not to wake the kind Americans in the motorboat next to us.

One of the main rules of a good yachtsman is never to drink alcohol while sailing or navigating by motor through the French Canals, but as we had allowed ourselves two days in the delightful town of Chalon-sur-Saône to have our regulator replaced, we had time to sober up and enjoy the sights and lovely friendly people before continuing our journey.

Friday 5th July 1986. We waved goodbye to our American friends who had told us we hadn't wakened them when we returned somewhat inebriated and they said they would be staying in Chalon-sur-Saône for a few more days before deciding to move on again.

Our next stop would be Tournus, so we filled our tank with water and set off with the sun shining down from a clear blue sky. It took all day to reach the peaceful mediaeval walled town, which was once a Roman Fort looking out over the Saône.

We tied up against the quay, followed by two English chaps in a very small 25' yacht that appeared to be very poorly equipped and very cramped for two people. We chatted to them and helped them tie up and they told us they had sailed from England in their little yacht. We admired their courage and adventurous spirit, and thereafter, whenever we thought

49

about them on our travels, referred to them as 'the intrepid pair'. We wondered what the French people would call their yacht, as it was so small. They called ours *Le petit bateau* so perhaps they would call their yacht *Le petit petit bateau!*

Leaving our new English friends to look for diesel and water, we set out to explore Tournus and were fascinated by the arcaded pavements and shops in the town centre selling delicious pâtisseries and épiceries.

We discovered Hôtel Dieu, which had served as a charity hospital until 1982. There had been three wards: one for women, one for men, and the other for soldiers all set around a chapel. Nearby the Musée Greuze displayed the works by the artist Jean-Baptiste Greuze (1725 - 1805) who was the son of the hospital's builder.

The Ancienne Abbaye Eglise St-Philibert was a huge building that we found at the other end of the town. It consisted of three churches built on top of each other in the course of a couple of centuries (9th - 11th) forming a single building in Romanesque style with castellations to repel attackers.

Alongside the Abbey, we found the Musée Bourguignon (Burgundy Museum) with a fine collection of displays on peasant life and folk costume.

Feeling hungry after our interesting morning discovering the history of this charming old-fashioned town, we came across a hotel-restaurant, but after our incident with the pig's trotters were rather wary when reading the menu which was purely in French. It described superb Burgundian cuisine – frog's legs, pig's trotters, and Bresse chicken. Needless to say, we avoided the frog's legs and pigs trotters and ordered the Bresse chicken that proved to be a gourmet's delight. We took note of it in case we came across it again in other restaurants on our travels.

By the time we had eaten our meal, it was getting on towards late afternoon and so we made our way to the town square where folk dancing was taking place. We were pleased that we had taken time to look into the town's history that day as we could better relate to the folk dancing and enjoyed trying to speak in our rusty French to the townspeople around us who obviously enjoyed joining in the town's frequent festivities.

Returning to the yacht feeling somewhat exhausted, we found great merriment was taking place on a pleasure barge which had moored just opposite us. We were invited aboard to take part in the festivities, but in view that we'd had a tiring but interesting day, we decided to give it a miss as tomorrow we were heading for our next stop... Mâcon.

Saturday 5th July 1986. We set out at 10am waving goodbye to all the holidaymakers on the pleasure barge who had invited us aboard the previous night. The weather was warm but stormy. Our intrepid friends said they would follow on later, so we were going to look out for them when we reached Mâcon. We had heard that it was a large industrial town in the centre of the region's wine trade, but had a riverside quay with lots of cafes, entertainment, shops and hotels where we hoped we could tie up for the night.

The weather continued to look stormy but it was warm so we enjoyed the journey arriving at the quay in Mâcon at about 2pm in the afternoon. Unfortunately, however, we were only allowed a brief stop because our yacht was considered too large to moor against the quay, whereas the 'intrepid pair' would be fine as their yacht was only 25' in length. Pleasure harbours were only for small craft we were told.

We stocked up with supplies from a nearby grocery store, phoned home to check on our three teenagers and found a delightful rustic style restaurant with a nice selection of dishes. We chose quenelles de brochet and Charolais beef. This would keep us going until we could find somewhere to moor for the night. The weather was not improving and so we made haste to return to the yacht and were sorry we were unable to see more of the town of Mâcon, which like most of the towns and villages we were encountering on our journey had a terrific history. Quite a number of historic buildings had survived the town's French Revolutionary fervour and we were disappointed we hadn't been able to visit the two museums. We had, however, bought some of the famous Mâcon wines - Mâcon Rouge and Mâcon Rosé.

As we untied from the mooring and prepared to leave, the weather worsened becoming very windy with rain beginning to fall quite heavily. We donned wet weather clothing, started the trusty Bukh engine, and headed out to find a suitable mooring for the night.

We came across a small quay where there were many pleasure craft tied up, but none the size of our yacht. When we attempted to tie up, we were told in no uncertain terms that it was only for small pleasure craft. We tried to explain in halting French that the weather was worsening and we needed to tie up for the night, but the mariner was adamant and told us to carry on.

The wind had built up by this time into a crescendo and the yacht was tossing from side to side. When looking over the side, we spotted water lilies and weeds around the keel of the yacht, so knew we were in the shallows and about to run aground… which we promptly did!

We were in quite a predicament with the weather worsening, pouring rain and nowhere to spend the night. We tried rocking the boat from side to side which had worked sometimes when we had run aground in the past, but it was refusing to budge and we were getting deeper and deeper into the mud.

Then, a small motorboat appeared through the pouring rain helmed by a small man shouting wildly in French. We thought he had come to tell us to move on, but he proved to be our benefactor. He promptly threw a warp to us and instructed us to tie it on to our cleat. He then tied the other end on his cleat and with some effort pushed his engine into first gear and tried pulling us out of the mud where we were deeply held by now. With much tearing and grinding of the gears and pulling on the rope, our yacht finally began to rise up out of the shallows into deeper water and away from the weeds and water lilies, but alas, our good friend lost his cleat as the force of pulling us out had been too much for a small boat.

We were very upset about this, as he had been so kind in helping us in our hour of need, but this was typical of the kindness that had been afforded us by all the people we had met. He told us not to worry about the cost... he had just been glad to help us.

Thankfully, we moved off again in the pouring rain endeavouring to keep in the centre of the canal looking for somewhere to tie up for the night. Just as it was getting dark, we discovered a village called Saint-Bernard and managed to moor along an old barge pontoon that was very high above us.

We were glad to get in out of the rain and cooked an evening meal, and then climbed into our bunks listening to it pitter-pattering on the coach roof all night interspersed by quite fierce thunderstorms.

Sunday 6th July 1986. Next morning, it was still raining, but undaunted we prepared the yacht and cast off, wearing our wet weather gear again. It was not the dull depressing rain with grey skies we have in England, so it was not a hardship, particularly as it was warm and blue skies were gradually peeping through the clouds.

The canal was narrow - more like a river - and we were surprised to see a lot of adults as well as children swimming in the water around us. A man riding his bicycle along the towpath spoke some English and told us they were sponsored swimmers racing to Trévoux. We carefully wound our way past them, ensuring the engine was in neutral.

We were heading for Lyon and chugged slowly along, enjoying the peacefulness of the beautiful countryside surrounding us, but by the time we were in sight of Lyon, the rain had started to come down in torrents and the wind had picked up whilst we were searching for a mooring.

We had hoped to see something of Lyon, particularly as we would be sailing through its namesake the Gulf of Lion. We had looked forward to savouring its gastronomical delights, as we had been told that the old streets were packed with modestly priced high quality restaurants called bouchons or mères. Also, Lyon is the third largest city in France, a World

Heritage Site and the second largest conurbation in France with excellent museums. It was originally Greek and before being occupied by the Romans.

It was Sunday, however, and when we arrived in the pouring rain, all the shops were closed and there was no sign of an area where we could tie up, and no chance at all of seeing the sights.

Disappointed, we soldiered on leaving Lyon behind undiscovered.

By this time a torrent was in full force and we knew we had to moor at the first convenient place we came to which was Pont Pasteur. We tied up alongside a Hotel at 2.30pm in the afternoon, and here again, as it was Sunday, all the shops were closed, but luckily, we still had supplies including diesel and water.

Chapter 8

Monday 7th July 1986. We knew that when we arose the next day we would be heading for the mighty river Rhône and that we should be stocked up and re-fuelled in preparation for the descent. On this passage, there would be no backwaters to escape from the current and passing wash of other traffic or provide shelter from the infamous mistral or Sirocco winds.

Along this river, the maximum boat dimensions were: height above waterline 6.3m, draught 3m with a speed limit of 30 km/h. There were 13 locks (190m long x 12m wide). We realised that the Rhône would be quite a challenge after days spent motoring at a leisurely walking pace, stopping for lunch, and mooring up early evening near a promising restaurant. In the space of a few days, we would have to cope with a strong current and pay a lot of attention to the weather when the boat was piloted down the waters of the fast moving Rhône sweeping towards the giant locks.

We were very thankful to see that the weather had slightly improved; we prepared the yacht in readiness to leave Pont Pasteur. It was still cloudy and not warm, so we donned sweaters, and with a feeling of apprehension, set out for the first lock.

We were delighted to see that when we arrived at the lock, our 'intrepid pair' in their 25' yacht were waving to us and looking very relaxed about tackling the first of these giant locks in their tiny craft. This gave us great confidence, and whilst we were all waiting for the lock to open to take us in alongside a huge barge, we handed them a cold beer for which they were extremely grateful.

When it was time for the lock to open, we went in together and tied up against the wall - waiting for the water to drop and gradually lower us into the deep abyss below. When the time came, one of the mariners released our warps and gently lowered us down - we were amazed at how simple it was. In fact, we thought it was a better operation than the smaller locks we had come through.

Our next port of call was Les Roches-de-Condrieu; it was 2pm when we pulled into a delightful marina. It was equipped with all facilities. For some reason most of the shops were closed on a Monday, but we eventually found a bread shop and boucherie to top up our supplies. The weather was still unsettled and clouds were scudding across the sky. We topped up with water, found some welcome showers, and scouted round for a telephone box to check on our three children. We were very low on diesel and so Brian managed to find the Marine Manager who said he would come to our yacht first thing in the morning to take him to the nearest diesel pump. We just hoped he would keep his word; otherwise, we couldn't risk departing for our next stop.

When we returned to the marina, we recognised the actor, Ronald Allen, on a motorboat named *Tania* from the television programme, *Crossroads*. *Tania* was moored just opposite, next to a yacht named *Compass*, owned by a British couple who lived in Spain. It was all rather cosy.

We looked around for a nice restaurant for our evening meal, but the only one recommended to us was a long way away on the other side of the bridge and very expensive, so we gave it a miss and had a glass of wine and cooked a meal on our gas cooker.

Tuesday 8th July 1986. True to his word, the Marina Manager knocked on our yacht at 8.30am in the morning and Brian took the jerry can to fill up with diesel, but didn't return for an hour, as the nearest pump was about a mile away on foot.

At 10am, we set off in convoy heading towards Valence with our newfound boating friends on *Tania* and *Compass*. The weather was still quite cold but by 11am had started to get warmer.

We reached Valence at 5.30pm and were pleased to see that it was a nice little yacht harbour with space for us to tie up. Our friends moored behind us. We wanted to look around Valence, which had a bright, busy river port with a tremendous history from Roman times. Originally known as Valentia Julia, the city was founded in 123 BC, but little now remains from those times - its historic ramparts having been replaced by boulevards 100 years ago. Despite this, we found it fascinating as we weaved our way through a tangle of little streets, known as cotes, lined with old houses. We visited the Musée de Valence which is in the former bishop's palace and learned that there was a house on Grande Rue on the worn façade of 16th century Maison des Têtes where large carved heads were displayed, representing the winds (fortune, time, theology, law and medicine). Another point of interest to us was that Napoleon lived opposite this house as a teenager student at the town's school of artillery. Another distinguished resident was François Rabelais (Renaissance writer, doctor, Renaissance humanist, monk and Greek scholar), who attended the university in the 15th century.

We had stocked up on diesel but realised we were running out of groceries, but came across a very large Casino hypermarket not far from the yachting marina. The only restaurant we came across was unfortunately very expensive; rumour has it that the Aga Khan and the King of Morocco, amongst other dignitaries, had dined there. Thus, we decided it was definitely not within our budget, so retreated to the yacht and dined on pizza and wine that was very pleasant sitting in the cockpit.

At some of the marinas with facilities, the mariners visited and wanted payment for mooring, but this was rare and generally, no one approached us for fees. Therefore, we prepared to leave next day to head for the next leg of our journey to Saint-Étienne-des-Sorts.

Wednesday 9th July 1986. The morning promised to be sunny and less windy as we rose at 7.30am in readiness for our journey. Our friends on *Compass* followed us as we went through the first lock together alongside a huge barge at 9.15am. By this time, we'd become very used to dealing with the locks and they presented no problems to us at all. At the second lock, we had to wait whilst barges and other craft went through, so we engaged in conversation with our friends on *Compass* shouting across the bows to one another amidst the whirring of engines. Another yacht, *Tantagel* from Guernsey in the Channel Islands, caught up with us in readiness to go through the lock at the same time, but by the time we were ready to go through at 11am, the wind had built up and the boats were leaping all over the place and we found *Ipi 'n tombia* difficult to handle. Her rigging was caught up against the wall, preventing the yacht from being lowered down as the water receded. Thankfully, a mariner spotted our dilemma and came along and kicked us free, otherwise we could have been hanging on to the wall with a deep drop below us.

We were quite relieved to find that once we were through the lock, our next stop was practically upon us, and we tied up at the quay wall at Saint-Étienne-des-Sorts behind a motorboat. The occupants were English and invited us aboard for drinks that evening and we told them we were heading for Aigues-Mortes, which they told us was a well-preserved fortified crusader port that sounded fascinating.

Thursday 10th July 1986. Our next port of call on our way to Aigues-Mortes was to be the well-known city of Avignon with its ancient town centre surrounded by its medieval ramparts. The weather was much improved so we donned shorts and T-shirts to soak up the sun. As we approached the first lock, we were sure to fix a stern line that made travelling through the lock easier. This time, we were going solo through the locks as we had now lost track of all the boating friends we had encountered on our journey through the canals.

We arrived at Avignon at 12.30pm and tied up at the quay, noticing that there were several nice looking restaurants nearby. We looked for water on the quay, which was difficult to find, as it was quite some distance away, but managed to extend our hosepipe and top up the water tank. There was no diesel pump in evidence and so we set out with our jerry can to find the nearest petrol station. It was quite a trek, however the garage attendant was most helpful and assisted us in filling up with diesel. These we put on a little trolley we used for the purpose and went back to the yacht ready to discover this beautiful city.

We hadn't realised it before, but we had arrived in Avignon at the most exciting time of the year, as France's largest festival takes place here from mid-July to mid-August at the magnificent Palais des Papes (Palace of the Popes). We learned that this had been the home until 1403 of the ten non-Roman popes. Disappointingly, we were to miss most of the festivities, as we had to move on next day to our final destination, Aigues-Mortes. This would be via Gallician in the Camargue, famous for its horses. After this, we were to return to England.

We did, however, have a delicious meal at a restaurant on the quay and sample the famous Châteauneuf-du-Pape - one of the finest wines of France from grapes grown in vineyards nearby.

Friday 11th July 1986. We experienced a blustery night, with the yacht bouncing around and Brian popping up to the deck every now and then to ensure the warps were tied safely. Next morning, however, the weather had chirped up again and it was bright and sunny. We prepared the yacht and motored slowly away from this very lovely city, feeling sorry we hadn't had time to join in the annual festivities or visit the museums to discover the history.

We were now heading for the Petit Rhône, which would mean that the locks would be smaller; we were amazed how easy they were to handle, and glad that we had left all the huge locks of the Rhône behind us. The sun continued to shine brilliantly from a clear blue sky and the terrain became flatter and verdant with the shadows of the trees and shrubs reflecting in the calm blue water.

Towards late afternoon, after a leisurely cruise drinking Oranginas to quench our thirst, we arrived in Gallician, a peaceful mooring against a grassy bank with fields all around us. We tied up and noticed a well-stocked grocery store nearby and a telephone box that meant we could check on our three children.

We met up with a couple called Rex and Alice from Scarborough, whom we had met previously on a motorboat and were pleased to see that they had caught up with us and were mooring behind us.

We invited them aboard for drinks when they had settled in. Whilst we were sitting in the cockpit, we noticed that there were three magnificent horses in the field across the way from our yacht and wondered if they were the famous horses of the Camargue region. Local fisherman waved to us in greeting as they sat quietly fishing on the riverbank and didn't seem too concerned when pleasure craft and barges passed by disturbing the waters.

Alice and Rex popped their heads out of their boat and asked if we were ready for them to come aboard and we made room for them in the cockpit. The sun was going down and it was very peaceful as we sat drinking our sundowners. There was, however, one fly in the ointment - or rather, several. As the sun went down, out came the mosquitoes, and some were quite vicious. In those days, we hadn't heard of the marvellous electric plug with a tablet, giving off an odour that mosquitoes don't like. Instead, we had to cope with the laborious job of putting up mosquito nets when the sun went down and plastering ourselves with repellent cream. Still, we did not complain, as we all considered it as a small price to pay for the opportunity of spending our days in paradise most of the time.

Saturday 12th July 1986. Our return to England was drawing close once again, so as much as we would have liked to stay in this delightful setting, we knew we had to move on in order to find a mooring for the winter months. Aigues-Mortes had been highly recommended to us.

We started the engine early in the morning and set out with our friends Alice and Rex following behind in their motorboat. The Petit Rhône proved to be a very relaxing and delightful river to navigate with lots of interesting things happening all the time on the towpaths as we motored by. We encountered several Safari Trip Land Rovers filled with tourists waving madly at us and shouting "Le petit bateau" as they sped off to some unknown terrain where we assumed they might find unusual species of wild animals!

Cyclists waved to us as they sped by, clutching French loaves and groceries - wobbling dangerously when we drew close to them. Families with children fishing on the bank cheered, and fishermen whistled and shouted. We felt quite like celebrities, but in the 1980's it was not a common sight to see a 10-metre yacht motoring through the French canals with the mast resting on the coach roof. Most of the craft were either barges or motorboats and that is why there was so much interest.

We eventually arrived at the walled town of Aigues-Mortes situated in a 13th Century Fortress, which we had been told was famous for its mediaeval history and the Crusades by King Louis IX. We felt as though we had arrived in the middle of nowhere and noticed about ten miles of natural beaches just behind the city. We found out later that these were protected by the national park of the Camargue. We also learned that Hannibal was believed to have set off with his elephants from Aigues-Mortes, though it was difficult to know how factual this was.

We arrived at the town quay at 11.30am but the charge to moor there - because it was a popular tourist area - would be 75 Frances per night. We had, however, been told we could tie up in the river just round the corner as the man who owned the land had the rights to moor several boats. We were very lucky indeed to have this opportunity as there was only one available space left.

The owner turned out to be quite a character by the name of Monsieur Fabre who called himself the Captain of the Moorings.

We left the yacht tied up at the quay, went across a bridge, and found his house situated just opposite the moorings where several motorboats and a couple of yachts were tied up. It looked as though it would be a safe mooring, sheltered from

61

the Mistral. It was reassuring to know that Monsieur Fabre's house overlooked the moorings and he obviously spent a lot of his time looking through the window. He was a portly gentleman partial to the anise-flavoured spirit, pastis, as were to find when we knocked on the door of his immaculate house.

His wife greeted us, invited us into the comfortable sitting room, and called to Monsieur Fabre who thankfully understood quite a bit of English. His wife immediately poured out the pastis and put some pistachio nuts in a tray at our side, which we had great difficulty in cracking, but we noticed Monsieur Fabre had mastered the art and was devouring the nuts. He finished his glass of pastis before we had even raised our glasses to our lips.

He told us he had been ill for quite some time and suffered with diabetes so we were not surprised when a very attractive nurse came in and told him it was time for his injection. We were told during our stay in Aigues-Mortes, that Monsieur Fabre had once cut a very dashing figure, and was considered the *ladies' man* of the town.

When the nurse left, we got down to business. Monsieur Fabre told us it would cost us £41 a month to moor our yacht, which we gratefully accepted and paid three months in advance.

He was reluctant to let us leave and told us about some of the history of Aigues-Mortes. He said it was built on saltpans - a strip of land between the town of Aigues-Mortes and the Mediterranean. Water is pumped into the Mediterranean and it then dries during the hot summer months. At the end of the summer, what is left in the saltpans becomes the salt used for roads and many other purposes.

We eventually managed to curtail our conversation as we had to move our yacht from the town wall round to our new mooring before we would be charged 75 Francs for the night.

We had just settled in when we were delighted to see our friends Rex and Alice had arrived at the Town Quay in their motorboat. We all decided to explore the town together, discovering many reasonably priced restaurants - it was hard to choose which one to patronise, as there was such a selection.

Sunday 13th July 1986. The next day was the eve of Bastille Day and, as we had missed the celebrations when we stopped at Sarry last year, we were determined to catch some of the celebrations here in Aigues-Mortes that were to take place that evening. We spent the day looking around the gypsy market where everything from food to exotic clothing, jewellery, and carpets could be bought. The sun was beating down and people of all nationalities were jostling one another to look at the various stalls and listen to the music being played by buskers sitting between the stalls - all hoping to receive a few franks for their efforts from the crowds.

After a fruit lunch at a nearby cute restaurant with red check tablecloths, we set off back to the yacht and showered in the cockpit with our plastic shower that we fixed up over the boom.

That evening we joined our friends, Alex and Rex, for a few drinks in the town square and joined in the Bastille festivities. These consisted of lots of fireworks and dancing – we arrived back at the yacht at 1am in the morning.

Monday 14th July 1986. We wandered over to the town square at about 10am hoping to see some more festivities, but all was quiet. We realised then that the festivities always took place in the evening; that was why we had missed them at Sarry - they had taken place the night before.

Undaunted, we decided to walk around the ramparts of the town which were about a mile long; this took up the rest of the morning. Feeling thirsty, we returned to the town square, had a couple of thirst-quenching beers, and returned to the yacht to eat lunch in the cockpit with the sun blazing down.

After our afternoon siesta, we decided to take the dinghy out and with the help of our trusty Yamaha outboard engine - we sailed around looking at the various yachts and motorboats in the town quay and surrounding area.

We were pleasantly surprised when we returned to the town square in the evening to see that the festivities were taking place once more with the addition of a fire-eater and a pop group with a female lead singer. She was attracting great attention from the crowds of boating people and tourists. This was followed by more firework displays and dancing in the square. Exhausted after joining in the dancing, we discovered Restaurant Le Galion and enjoyed a delightful meal for the price of 53 Francs each.

Tuesday 15th July 1986. We decided to explore the surrounding area by train, and for the price of 17 Francs for the two of us, we set out for the next port - Le Grau-du-Roi - a coastal commune in the Gard department of Southern France. We thought we might be able to moor our yacht here prior to moving off into the notorious Gulf of Lion on our way to Spain.

We didn't think it was as quaint as Aigues-Mortes; it was more touristy, but it was right on the beach. We found the Tourist office and caught a bus to nearby Port Camargue - a lovely yacht harbour. Many of the yachts and motorboats were moored at the bottom of delightful little apartments so that the owners could step out of their doors and sail off in their craft. The cost of the apartments was just £35,000 and thus we were very tempted to up sticks in England and move to Port Camargue!

We found a nice little restaurant for lunch and waved to our friends Alice and Rex as they motored past on their way to the Mediterranean. We would miss them as we had enjoyed their company for several days, but the joy of cruising was that you met many acquaintances on your journey, and it was quite likely that you'd bump into them again somewhere.

On our return to Le Grau-du-Roi, we decided to test out the beach and went swimming in the sea. We found it to be surprisingly cold considering the heat of the day.

At the end of the day, we returned to the train station, only to find there was trouble on the line and there were no trains back. We waited a couple of hours before finally a bus going in the direction of Aigues-Mortes turned up. Another joy in cruising is that we had all the time in the world and each happening usually turned into an adventure.

We visited one of the supermarkets in the town square in Aigues-Mortes and decided to have a barbecue on the yacht after purchasing juicy steaks and a bottle of fine red wine.

Wednesday 16th July 1986

Our time for returning to England had arrived and we had a problem in not knowing what to do about a life raft. This is vital equipment for a sailor, particularly as we would be crossing the Gulf of Lion on our next trip. Eventually, we decided to purchase one, but it cost £1,000. We decided that although we could barely afford it, it was better than risking our lives, particularly as that night the wind blew up with a vengeance. We wondered what it would be like in the Gulf if we were caught in the grips of the blustery Mistral - but that would not be until July next year.

Chapter 9

France to Spain - 28th July 1987. The Mediterranean Spanish coast stretches from the Strait of Gibraltar to the border with France in the Gulf of Lion. The coastline is approximately 750 miles long and has traditionally been divided into five 'costas' which split the coast into Costa Brava, Costa Dorada, Costa del Azahar, Costa Blanca, and Costa del Sol.

The Costa Brava extends from Rio Tordera for 67 miles to the French Border. This is a mountainous coastline, and tourism is not as heavy here as on the other costas.

Costa Dorada - the golden coast - extends from Cabo Tortosa for 140 miles to Rio Tordera, the name derived from the many fine golden sandy beaches along its coastline. It is now developed for tourism and has been dubbed 'the great wall of Spain'.

Costa del Azahar extends from Cabo de San Antonio for 115 miles to Cabo Tortosa. The coast is known as the orange blossom coast from the numerous citrus orchards along the coast. Tourism is not so heavy here.

Costa Blanca - the White Coast - extends nearly 200 miles from Cabo de Gata to just beyond Cabo de San Antonio. The coast is bordered by high white cliffs (hence the name) and tourism is now very popular.

The Costa del Sol – the sunny coast - is the most popular coast for tourism and extends from the Strait of Gibraltar for 155 miles to Cabo de Gata. It is mostly flat near the coast, although high mountains are a short distance inland.

A year had passed since we had done very much sailing, although we had visited Aigues-Mortes a few times to ensure our yacht was safe. Our son and his friend, Barrie, enjoyed two weeks holiday there looking after the yacht and seeing the sights, but in June 1987 we received a phone call to say that the mooring was no longer available to us, as Monsieur Fabre was no longer there. We didn't know what had happened to him but Brian had to fly out to see if he could take the yacht to another mooring.

He remembered that we had visited the port of La Grau-du-Roi, so single handed, he motored from Aigues-Mortes in the direction of the port hoping to find a safe haven for the yacht until we were ready to head for the Mediterranean and our final destination on the Costa del Sol in Spain.

The port was full of boats of all descriptions, but Brian tied up against the quay alongside some fishing boats and went in search of the Mariner. The Mariner turned out to look very much like *The Hulk* from the TV series of the time being broadcast in the UK. He agreed to let him tie up against the quay until July when we would be heading for the notorious Gulf of Lion, so he made the yacht safe and headed back to the UK to prepare for our major journey to Spain.

Full of excitement on July 28th 1987, we flew to France and made our way to La Grau-du-Roi to prepare *Ipi 'n tombia* in readiness for our trip. We enjoyed a relaxing day swimming on the beach and eating ice cream in the little café overlooking the boatyard where the yacht was still tied up against the quay.

Our friend - *The Hulk*, as we remember him to this day - greeted us. We paid our dues and prepared to cast off, but there was such a confusion of warps all mixed up together, that Brian did an unforgivable thing - he cut the ropes with his knife to cast us free of the quay. The alternative was to stay there all day trying to untie them. At last, engine running and our onboard music player blasting out the theme from *Ipi Tombi*, we sped away from the port. We tried not to look back, as there was an angry *Hulk* jumping up and down on the quay looking at the cut ropes.

It was just 8am local time with a clear blue sky and a wind of force 4-5. We thought we would have a reasonably calm passage across the Gulf, despite tales we'd heard of the famous cold, blustery katabatic wind named, the Mistral. The Gulf of Lion is a wide embayment of the Mediterranean coastline of Languedoc-Roussillon and Provence in France, reaching from the border with Catalonia in the west to Toulon.

67

The chief port on the Gulf is Marseille, with Toulon also important, and a favourite with the hake fishermen. There was, however, a decline in the business from over-fishing.

We'd heard so much about the notoriety of the bay and that the name does not come from the lion, but rather from the city of Lyon, the ancient capital of the Gauls. Lyon, which we had passed on our way through the canals, is on the Rhône River and empties into the Gulf. The name had evolved during the Middle Ages from Lugdunum to Loudoun, and then to Lion.

After motoring through the canals, it felt good to be setting our sails and at last putting out to sea and. For a while it was paradise, with the wind in the sails and the hot sun beating down as we sat in the cockpit - I on the tiller and Brian tending the mainsail and jib.

Our newfound paradise, however, was not to last long, as the wind later gusted to force 6 with a rougher sea building up. As the wind strengthened, we knew that we were going to have to cope with the dreaded Mistral, and Brian asked me whether I wanted to turn round and go back to Le Grau-du-Roi. The prospect of an angry *Hulk* waiting to greet us, however, did not appeal. We pressed on.

The wind grew so strong that we decided to take down the sails and proceed under motor alone. The sea state transformed into huge waves; it was rather like being on a roller coaster at the fairground - only scarier.

I was feeling decidedly queasy and resorted to being sick in the scuppers. Seasickness can be bad, but I never really knew just how bad until then. I felt past caring about anything other than to get back on to dry land.

Worse was to happen. At about 2am in the morning it was pitch black and the engine spluttered to a definite halt, so we were left with just the sails to rely on to guide us across the bay. The swell was so high that it was impossible to go up on to the deck to put up the main and the jib, as in those days, we didn't have roller reefing on the jib. We knew that something had to be done, so Brian waited for a break in the wind and clipped on to the safety lines, struggling forward in an endeavour to put up the jib. He eventually managed to raise the sail after a great deal of effort and stumbling around on the foredeck.

The wind eventually died down, but the swell remained high; the yacht leapt up and down and my seasickness was worsening all the time. With the engine gone and the mainsail out of action, we realised we were in trouble.

The sky was as black as ink and the stars felt so near-almost as if you could reach out and touch them. If it had been a calm night with no swell, it would have been a remarkable sight, but we were by then extremely tired and strange things happen at sea when you are tired. Beacons on the hill in the far distance appeared to have scaffolding around them (which, of course they didn't), and strange objects danced before our eyes, so we knew somehow we would have to try to get ashore.

To add to our woes, we heard the dreaded sound of a huge ship's throbbing engines heading nearer. Worst of all, both port and starboard lights indicated that it was heading straight for us. I was being sick in the scuppers and past caring when Brian said, "take this torch and wave it up and down for all you are worth!" He then put all the cabin lights on. We had no engine to guide us away from the ship; we could only pray that they would see the feeble torch light and the light from our cabin windows.

God was in his heaven that night - mercifully, the lights on the ship indicated a change in direction, and it headed away from us, leaving us leaping up and down on the swell once again.

I took the tiller and tried to guide the yacht in a direction I thought it should go, whilst Brian wrapped himself up in a blanket in the cockpit and went to sleep. This, as it happened, was a sensible thing to do although I didn't agree with him at the time. The jib helped us to head in the right direction, the wind had died down, and most of the time we spent wallowing in the steep waves. We could at last see a rocky coastline as dawn was breaking - we were passing Cabo-Creus. But getting past the point was proving difficult when sailing under jib alone. After a mammoth effort, we finally achieved it, and noticed a little island between some rocks in the distance. We steered towards it and, miraculously, worked our way between the rocks at 12 noon, albeit feeling totally exhausted.

By this time, the sun was up and we thought we had landed in heaven. We didn't realise it then, but we had ventured into the small bay on the Cap de Creus peninsula on the Costa Brava, namely Port Lligat. Yachts and small motorboats were bobbing up and down on the sparkling clear blue sea, and it was not long before we realised it was a naturist area - none of the owners of the boats wore any clothes. They were completely naked, happily going about the tasks on their boats, or swimming lazily in the sea. It was as if we had entered another world. We wondered if we were dreaming - perhaps we'd capsized at sea and had now arrived in heaven.

Friendly naked yachts people, mainly French, helped us to anchor and the water was so clear we could see the anchor chain settling right down on the seabed. Everyone was very friendly and offered to help, but we found it quite embarrassing as we were dressed in shorts and tops, whilst they were all naked. There was no way either of us were going to discard our clothes.

We thanked them all profusely for their help and collapsed in the cabin to enjoy a long sleep after our rather terrible adventure across the Gulf of Lion that we would never forget.

Next morning, we were awakened by a knocking on the hull of the yacht and were greeted by a German lady swimming in the water alongside. She asked if we wanted to join her and her husband for breakfast. We thought it was very kind of her, but we made a hasty excuse as we had noticed she was stark naked and we might be expected to take off our clothes for morning breakfast.

We decided to get out our *Bombard* dinghy and head ashore to see whether we could find a mechanic to look at our *Bukh* engine, as we wouldn't be able to proceed down the coast until it was fixed. I showered in the cockpit in my swimsuit and felt quite out of place looking at everyone swimming around and having breakfast in his or her cockpits with no clothes on.

Whilst we were enjoying our breakfast, we noticed a French man on the cliff at the side of the bay completely naked and posing in a very 'Bruce Forsyth' fashion. Soon after, a 42' French yacht came into the bay with a crew of about six people who had hardly put down anchor before they stripped off all their clothes and dived into the water.

We wondered whether the local inhabitants of the nearby village would be wandering around with no clothes on. We sincerely hoped not, there was only so much of this we could take!

We lowered our dinghy over the side of the yacht, started the engine, and headed towards the rocky shore where we left it. Everywhere in France had been safe; so far, no one had endeavoured to steal either our dinghy or the engine, so we hoped that the Spanish people would be as honest as the French would.

We found the village of Cadaqués just over the hill from the bay of Port Lligat, to be fascinating and thankfully, the locals wore clothes. We looked around for a mechanic's yard and a shop to stock up with groceries. We didn't have much luck in finding anything remotely like a garage, but did find a little wooden shack that sold diesel fuel. Here, we had to switch from the French language to Spanish, which did prove easier as I had been working in Spain for quite a while prior to our setting out in the yacht and had picked up a smattering of the language.

In the 1980's when we discovered Cadaqués, it was not a tourist town, but by 2002, it had grown with a population of 2,612 people. Artist Salvador Dalí often visited the area in his childhood, and quite unexpectedly on our way back to the yacht, we came across his, recognisable by two stone sculptures of giant eggs outside. The house had been converted into a museum: the Casa-Museo Salvador Dalí. Both the bay of Port Lligat and the island have been represented in several of Dalí's paintings such as *The Madonna of Port Lligat* and *The Sacrament of the Last Supper*.

We learned that *The Madonna of Port Lligat* is the name of three paintings by Salvador Dalí. The first was created in 1949, the second in 1950, and with the same title and theme now exhibited by the Fukuoka City Art Museum, Japan. The paintings both depict a seated Madonna with baby Jesus on her lap. Dalí's wife, Gala, posed for these pictures.

We were fascinated by this eccentric artist and later discovered a lot of information about his background and history.

Born Salvador Domingo Felipe Jacinto Dalí i Domènech on May 11, 1904 in Figueres, Catalonia, he died on January 23rd, 1989, aged 84. One of his best-known works *The Persistence of Memory* was completed in 1931. He claimed that his ancestors were descended from the Moors, which may have contributed to his grandiose behaviour that drew much attention to himself as an eccentric character.

We had not expected our search for a mechanic to result in the discovery of the house of this famous artist; we vowed to return to learn more once we had sorted out our engine.

Our dinghy remained where we'd left it on the beach, so wondering how we could repair the engine, we returned to the yacht to find that it had slipped its anchorage. Fortunately, two friendly Germans (naked of course), had moved it and made it secure. They offered to row ashore and look for a mechanic for us. We thought this was very generous, but we hoped they would put some clothes on first.

We were relieved to see that they disappeared into their respective yachts and their wives appeared fully clothed, started up their dinghy, waved to us and said they would go in search of a mechanic for us.

In the meantime, a French yacht had anchored close by to us and in halting English, the crew consisting of two naked Frenchmen, asked us if they could help with our engine. We said we would be grateful and would pay them for their time, but they were adamant they didn't want payment. Fellow yachtsmen always helped one another, as they all knew that equipment failure at sea could sometimes be a matter of life and death.

They came over to our yacht dressed in shorts, removed the engine housing, and discovered that the problem was the fuel pump. In no time, they had put it right and the sound of the engine running sweetly was music to our ears. Having noted that the Frenchmen smoked, we handed them a big pack of cigarettes that we had kept for the lockkeepers, and they seemed very pleased. We were a bit concerned about our German ladies who had gone off to see if they could find a mechanic to come to the boat, but we were relieved to see that they were on the way back in their dinghy - like ourselves, they'd had no luck in finding one. We thanked them profusely for their efforts, and at the same time hoped they wouldn't invite us aboard their yacht for drinks, just in case they chose to be naked.

That night proved to be very windy and the anchor didn't hold. We managed to get a line on to the nearby French yacht and discovered that our ground gear was not good enough for that particular bay.

The north west Tramontana wind was still blowing the next day, so we went into Cadaqués, taking our trolley and diesel can to top up with four gallons of fuel ready for the journey down the coast. We now had eight gallons that would last for quite some time if we could get some good sailing in without relying on the engine.

We hoped that we could move off the next day, but now the Mistral was blowing to a near gale, but was forecast to stop on Sunday 2nd August.

We were anxious to move on, as we had to find a permanent mooring prior to returning to England to take up our respective jobs again. We had been told that Empuriabrava situated on the coast of Girona, Catalonia, was a beautiful place and one of the largest marinas in the world.

2nd August 1987. True to the forecast, the weather was bright and sunny as we set out heading for Empuriabrava - it felt like paradise. We had long ago decided that sailing long distance was either paradise or a living hell! There seemed to be no happy medium.

The yacht moved smoothly through the water with our trusty Bukh engine functioning well again, and a gentle breeze was filling the sails with the sun beating down from a clear blue sky. We sat in the cockpit with Brian tending the sails and me on the tiller and keeping an eye on the compass. We didn't have the luxury of satellite navigation in those days; we navigated by means of the various pilot books (for each Costa in Spain), relying heavily on our binoculars so that we could spot the ports and various landmarks. The torres (towers) on the rugged coastline proved to be of great value in establishing our position. They were built by the Moors in the Middle Ages to warn of impending landings or the presence of enemy ships. We noticed that there were many of them, all within sight of one another in order to communicate by smoke signals, and later by canon.

At last, we were feeling the joys of sailing the Mediterranean in beautiful sunshine with a relatively calm sea, acknowledging passing yachts and motorboats, some out for day sailing, and others like ourselves heading towards exciting unknown destinations.

We arrived at the entrance to Empuriabrava in the late afternoon. Situated in the Bay of Rosas, it was built on land that, until forty years ago, was all farmland dating back to the 14th century.

As we approached, we entered a man-made canal with residential homes on each side and boats moored at the bottom of their gardens. We eventually reached the marina that was situated opposite the residential houses. Luxury yachts and motorboats, both large and small, jostled against each other in the gentle swell of the canal.

We went in search of the Capitán's office to see if we could book a mooring for a year. On the way, we noticed that attempts had been made to build a swimming pool and restaurants, but it looked much neglected and only half completed. All around us, members of the boating fraternity were bustling around tending their various vessels and calling in greeting to one another in different languages. We asked a German man whether he could direct us to the Capitán's office; he introduced himself and kindly accompanied us to the office. He told us he was mooring in the marina for six months and that it was a very good, although somewhat expensive.

As was the system in those days, we sat in front of the Capitán and negotiated the best price we could for mooring the yacht for twelve months. The length and width of the yacht was important in how much was charged. We were fortunate since *Ipi 'n tombia*, being a racer/cruiser sleek narrow lines, meant that the width was favourable - though she was still 10 metres in length. After a good amount of haggling, we negotiated a fair price and went off to the mooring we had been allocated.

We were amazed to find that we were moored next to *Alice E* - our friends Alice and Rex whom we had met on the canals. They had motored across the Gulf of Lion in calm seas, avoiding the Mistral winds we had experienced, and without the trauma we had encountered. They had reached Empuriabrava ahead of us.

After much celebration at the local café that night, we settled down to enjoy a week in this beautiful marina that, according to the café owner, was in the process of being turned into a resort for wealthy tourists, offering tennis, water and aerial sports. During our stay, however, there was not much of this in evidence, apart from many shops in the commercial area, and as we were to discover later - beautiful beaches.

It seemed strange that in the early 1960's when the rest of Spain was experiencing the first major tourism boom, this area was still an agricultural community unsure of what tourism would do to its way of life.

During our week in Empuriabrava, we ventured out of the marina to do some sailing, as the weather was calm. Although a Mistral had been forecast, it didn't materialise. We sailed out beyond the point of the bay where the wind was stronger and enjoyed some good fast sailing. We planned to sail one night to practice, as we hadn't enjoyed our last experience in darkness in the Gulf of Lion. It was a pity to have bad memories, as we'd heard that sailing in the Mediterranean at night could be wonderful. We chose a balmy, still evening, motored out of the bay, put up the sails, and switched the engine off. We were not disappointed. There was no sound other than gentle waves lapping against the hull and a mild breeze rustling through the sails. The stars reached down to us from a pitch black sky - so close you felt you could almost reach out and touch them. This was indeed another paradise... much different to the night we had spent leaping about in the Gulf with no engine.

The breeze gradually built up to a 3 - 4 with small waves, which was just right; the yacht was speeding along merrily.

This was a perfect ending to our brief stay in Empuriabrava, and the next day we prepared to return once again to our life in England.

Chapter 10

The Southampton Boat Show was taking place in September that year and after our experience in the Gulf of Lion, we decided we really should have roller reefing. This would mean that if we had to endure heavy seas, we could handle the foresail from the cockpit. We also decided that we needed a mainsail that would be easier to handle and so bought the 'Dutchman' reefing system, that folds the sail neatly when lowered, rather than our conventional mainsail - that tended to drop over our heads, and all over the deck when trying to take it down. We were in danger of becoming completely enfolded in the sail if there was a strong wind, and that was no joke.

We also bought other bits and pieces for the yacht, but then wondered how we would transport all this new equipment to Spain. We decided we would drive through France in our new Metro car. This would be a nice experience, and we could meet all our friends on the marina again before they departed to their various destinations. We managed to take time off work, packed the sails, a new EPIRB (Emergency Position Indicating Radio Beacon), and VHF radio into the car, and took it in turns to drive through France and then on to the Costa Brava in Spain.

It was an interesting trip and made easy by the fabulous peajes (toll roads). The French countryside was breathtaking, and we stayed for one night in a small pension situated on the side of a narrow road. The bedroom was very tiny, with a shower in the cupboard. Despite the modest accommodation, the breakfast next morning was delicious - served by a friendly waitress who had lived in London for a while and spoke some English.

Our one disappointment in France was the state of the toilets at the various stops along the motorways. They consisted mainly of just a hole in the ground and no differential between the sexes. They were dirty and the doors didn't close, so it resulted in people heading off into the bushes, which wasn't very satisfactory.

Thankfully, this problem was resolved as we approached Paris. It was good to see the city again and we fondly remembered the island just off the Seine that we moored at during our travels through the canals. We had not experienced driving in the city until this point, and found it positively hair-raising, with traffic converging on us from all directions as we drove down the Champs-Elysées.

We travelled on beyond the city and the journey became straightforward from then on - arriving in Empuriabrava in good time to park the car and make our way with excitement to our yacht mooring.

As we approached our yacht with our arms full of bags, we were greeted by with great pleasure by Alice and Rex who helped us settle in. Although we were very tired after our journey, we didn't feel we could refuse their offer to go out to dinner. They had been so kind to us, so we accompanied them with some German boating friends of theirs.

We found ourselves dining in a typical German restaurant eating piles of mashed potatoes and sauerkraut - not ideal for a good night's sleep after a long journey. Needless to say, we joined in German drinking songs, scoffed German beer, and staggered back to the yacht, collapsing into our bunks to fall asleep immediately.

We only had a few days in which to put up our new sails, try out our new Bombard dinghy (which we had bought at the boat show) and fit our new radio, so we were up very early. Breakfasting in the cockpit, we noticed that there was no sign of Alice and Rex who were still sound asleep on their boat.

We sauntered along the quay heading in the direction of our car and wondered how we were going to get all our new gear onto the quay and onto the yacht. Our problem was solved when one of the mariners passed by, noticed our dilemma, and offered to put everything on to his truck and drive it to our yacht on the quay. We thanked him profusely and took up the offer. He not only helped us put the sails and dinghy on to his truck, but also made sure they were all safely aboard our yacht before he went on his way, and refused point blank to take any money for his kindness.

By this time, there was a stirring from *Alice E* next door and Rex popped his head out through the hatch to ask if we wanted any assistance in putting up the sails - he knew many people who would help us. We gratefully accepted their offer and in no time, six willing yachtsmen surrounded our yacht all speaking in different languages. The one saving grace was that they were all experienced yachts people, so knew how to set the roller reefing and 'Dutchman' reefing systems. The job was finished by mid-day and I fished out some beer from a cool box that was swimming in water due to the hot sun beating down. In those days, we didn't have a fridge, and ice didn't last very long. Nevertheless, everyone sat in the cockpit drinking their beer and saying how much they had enjoyed helping us.

We were thrilled that at last we had a jib that we could control from the cockpit and no longer have to scrabble forward on deck in bad weather. The mainsail would also be a lot easier to manage, although we would still have to balance on the cabin roof to hoist it and bring it down. But now it would fold neatly and not be in danger of enveloping us as it had done before.

We couldn't wait to try them out, so set out next morning for a gentle sail in the bay. There was a breeze of between force 3 - 4 with small waves. We were amazed at how easy it was to sail with roller reefing - just a matter of slowly unfurling the foresail until it was fully open and then if the breeze got too strong we could furl it back in to decrease the sail area. The mainsail behaved itself a lot better too and didn't put us in danger of being entangled in it.

We enjoyed a leisurely few days swimming and enjoying the companionship of Alice and Rex and other friends in the area. One couple had set out from Brighton in England in their *Westerley* yacht and, like us, had motored through the French Canals. I noticed that their yacht was immaculate inside and there were even plants in pots in the cockpit. We feared that they wouldn't last long when sailing in the Mediterranean, as the slightest chop or swell would see them scattering all over the cockpit floor.

We planned to visit Empuriabrava againin the winter months, before June when we would sail on to our next destination. We thought it would be interesting to see what the marina would be like in winter.

When we returned in December, however, it was a much different scene to the summer. *Alice E* had moved on, as had our friends with the plant pots in the *Westerley*, and there was no one about whom we recognised. The marina appeared to be totally deserted with the town of Empuriabrava felt a bit like a ghost town.

We had flown into Girona Airport and taken a taxi to the marina so did not have a car; we were virtually stranded on the marina with not a lot to do other than do some repairs, clean the cabin, and scrub the decks. Although quite chilly, the sun shone during the daytime enabling us to have breakfast and lunch in the cockpit, so it was not all doom and gloom.

During this time, I was involved in the sale of property in the area east of Malaga on the Costa del Sol, and received a phone call from a very nice lady from Leigh-on-Sea, not far from Canvey Island. She said that she and her husband wanted to leave England and live in Spain permanently and would I take her out on a three-day trip to view property. Establishing that she was serious about buying, and had the money available if she found a property to suit, I arranged to meet her with her husband in Nerja - the area she was interested in buying.

Abandoning my 'yachting hat' I put my 'property selling hat' on, hired a car, and drove to Barcelona where I caught a plane to Málaga. I picked up a hire car at Málaga and drove to Nerja and the very beautiful El Capistrano villages situated on the outskirts of the town. Here, I found a lovely villa for them with views out to sea, located near to the communal pool. I loved the work I was doing during those days as I was interspersing my selling career with my leisure activity, and discovered that you can mix business with pleasure. I was pleased that I had found a nice property for the couple from

Leigh-on-Sea, and after ensuring they caught their flight back to England, I flew back to Barcelona where Brian met me with a hire car. He said it had been dead everywhere whilst I had been away and cold on the yacht in the evenings.

We decided to pack up and leave for England again the next day, as no restaurants were open and very few shops open for groceries. In the 1980's Empuriabrava Marina was only just beginning to form into a tourist area and there were not enough people living locally to sustain it through the winter months. Cafés, restaurants, shops and bars had to make enough money during the summer months in order to survive.

Our next trip was to be in June 1988 and so we headed back to work in readiness for our next adventure.

Chapter 11

June 6th, 1988. We hadn't visited *Ipi 'n tombia* since our trip in December and were looking forward to some nice warm sunshine this time. As much of my work was done in Spain, Brian decided he would retire from his job and assist me. This would provide us with an income and a lot of time to spend sailing - we even made plans to join the ARC heading to Las Palmas in the Canary Islands in November. We could then join a group of about 200 yachts heading for St Lucia in the Caribbean. But first, we had the Mediterranean to tackle.

We set out full of anticipation, armed with big bags of items such as First Aid equipment, batteries, some items of food not obtainable at that time in Spain, and various tools for emergency repairs, which hopefully wouldn't be too many. We flew into Girona airport and spotted a taxi; the driver came over and helped us with our heavy bags. He disregarded any rules the Marina might have had about driving cars on the pontoons and drove us right up to our yacht. He then proceeded to help us to load our bags aboard, so we thanked him with a big tip and he went off whistling quite happily.

Now the summer months were upon us and we noticed that the marina, unlike the winter period, was packed full of vessels - there was very little room for any other yachts or motorboats to moor. As we would be leaving the next day, however, it would mean that there would be a spare mooring for another yacht of our size.

As we were preparing to settle down for the night, we noticed a sailing yacht cruising up and down the pontoons looking for a space. As we knew there was nowhere for them to go, we flagged the skipper down and told him he could raft up against us for the night until we left in the morning. They were a very nice French couple who reminded us a lot of Pierre and Nicole whom we had shared part of the canals journey. They were very grateful to raft up, as they were exhausted due to the

Mistral which had blown up and caused choppy seas – this didn't auger well for us setting out the next day.

We found as we journeyed through the Mediterranean that it was necessary to raft up when the ports were busy, otherwise there could be nowhere to moor. Yachting people mostly understood that this was necessary, but there were many who tried to avoid it, which wasn't fair on their fellow yachtsman. Rafting up required a line to be thrown to another yacht and made secure fore and aft, so that the yachts were moored side by side. In this configuration, occupants would often have to step aboard other yachts in order to go ashore, so quite often in the middle of the night there could be quite a disturbance when people crossed to get to their yacht, particularly if several were rafted up together.

We rose early the next morning and went to see the Capitán to tell him we were leaving, and that a French couple would be in our mooring and wished to stay for a while. We were sorry to leave Empuriabrava as it was one of the nicest marinas on the Costa Brava even though it was as dead as a doornail during the winter months.

The weather looked unsettled with a wind force 3 - 4 gusting to 5 and the seas were quite rough, but we had given up our mooring and had no choice but to continue along the coast. As soon as we came out into the bay, however, we realised just how rough the seas were and the new mainsail was quickly pulled away from the boom by a vicious gust of wind. Aware that we no longer had a mooring in Empuriabrava, we decided we had no choice but to return to the port and so headed back in under motor and jib. We were lucky enough to find a space to moor for the night whilst we put the new mainsail back to rights.

The weather forecast for the next day sounded better, blowing 3 - 4 with good visibility and the possibility of rain that evening, so prepared to leave at 8am in order that we could reach our next stop in good time.

We motored out, finding the sea remaining choppy and the weather unsettled, but we soldiered on. As was the case the previous day, the wind blew to force 5 - 6, and the mainsail pulled out of the slot again - we obviously didn't have the knack of connecting new one on to the boom. We decided to head for a little bay named Cala Montgó at the southern tip of the Bay of Rosas to fix it. The bay extends three kilometres inland from the shoreline and includes the hills of Roca Maura and Torre Moratxa. The weather was deteriorating rapidly, and as we attempted to fit the old mainsail to the boom, three brutal squalls hit us in quick succession, knocking the yacht over - we feared a capsize. Brian managed to roll in the foresail with the roller reefing whilst shouting instructions to me. I was to bring the yacht under control by steering her into the wind at each squall, saving us from further knockdowns, or a dreaded capsize. The squalls were gusting force 8 - 9, building momentum and funnelling between the hills, so it had perhaps not been a very wise decision to stop in the bay to change the sail.

Once we had fitted our old mainsail between the squalls, we headed out to open sea, setting a course towards the Illes Medes - a small and craggy group of seven islets in the northwestern Mediterranean. In more favourable weather, this would have been worth a visit as it is a world-renowned diving paradise of uninhabited islands. Protected by Natural Park status, the islands are home to many different species of flora and fauna, above and below water.

Once out in the open sea, the rig was back in working order with our old mainsail back in place on the boom. The sea was very choppy but with the sails trimmed we were making good headway - with the wind in the sails and the sound of the spray rushing beneath us, it was exhilarating as *Ipi 'n tomiba* sped through the waves.

We had thought of stopping at L'Estartit, which today is a small town and seaside resort situated between the foothills of the Montgri Massif and the Mediterranean Sea. In the 1980's, however, it was just a small fishing village with very few villas or shops, so we decided to keep going as we were make good way and the wind was in the right direction for good sailing.

We passed by Palamos situated at the northern end of a large bay. Popular now for swimming, sailing, and windsurfing, today it is a major port surrounded by bars and restaurants. In those days, this too was just a small fishing village, but grew upon the closure of Sant Feliu de Guíxols, the only commercial harbour in the Province of Girona.

The wind had died down to a gentle breeze by 4pm that afternoon and, as we had enjoyed some excellent sailing, we decided to carry on through the night towards Blanes. It proved to be a blissful sail with a clear sky and brilliant moon shining on the water - guiding us towards our destination. The stars were very bright in the night sky and the silence was complete, almost eerie, apart from the gentle sound of water rippling past our hull as we cut through the gentle waves. We took it in turns to sleep and take the tiller, arriving at Blanes at 8am the next morning feeling refreshed.

There was no marina at Blanes, so we tied up against the quay alongside a German and French yacht whose owners were either still asleep or absent as no-one appeared to help us, as was usual case when a yacht arrived to tie up. We breakfasted in the cockpit and went off to discover the area and found some lovely beaches surrounded by steep rocky cliffs and small coves. We enjoyed a swim and then explored the small town, eventually relaxing at a pavement café where we enjoyed a café con leche and tostada before heading back to the yacht. The café owner told us the name of Blanes was also the name of a horse circus that travelled up to the North of Europe, eventually ending up in Amsterdam. We thought this a strange, yet interesting, gem of wisdom to impart to us.

We noticed something was not quite right about the way *Ipi 'n tombia* was lying against the quay as we approached to climb on board. We then realised one of our large fenders was missing, also the two yachts which had been tied up next to us, had gone. We had no doubt that one of them had taken our fender. This is a rare happening amongst yachtsmen. Usually, they are more than helpful and strictly honest, as we all know that yachting is a serious business and help from other crews could save a life. We were quite upset to think that something from the yacht had been stolen. It was, however, the only time it happened in all of the years we spent cruising the Spanish coast.

During my phone call to check on the children the next morning, they told me that I had had an enquiry from a client who wanted to purchase a warehouse and big villa in the area of Salou. Once again, I was going to have to mix business with pleasure. I knew a very well respected Spanish family in Salou who owned several commercial properties, as well as residential properties in the vicinity, so I contacted them to find out what was available. I then called the client who told me he was visiting Salou within the next few days. If we could manage to get there, I would be able to make the introduction to my contact; my client could then choose a property to live in with his wife and three children, together with a warehouse to store goods.

We had intended mooring at Barcelona on the way and having a look around the city, but now time would not allow if we were to arrive in Salou to meet my client. It was full speed ahead. We were fascinated by the massive harbour at Barcelona as we passed by. In some ways, though, we were glad we didn't have to navigate our way in to find a mooring, as large ships were passing in and out on a regular basis.

Chapter 12

Costa Dorada. After some fast sailing, we arrived at Tarragona and found the yacht club located at the end of the port with its own yacht harbour, club premises, restaurant, and a café. We had no difficulty in finding a mooring and went to the restaurant to enjoy a good meal. We learned that the Royal Tarragona Yacht Club had quite a history as it was first established in 1878. We were very amused to hear that at that time it was locally known as Club del Xiflats ("Club of the dim-witted" in Catalan). At that time, none of the local people could understand why members of the club wanted to sail; they considered it the arduous task of fishermen who often risked their lives at sea just to make a catch for a living!

We wished we could have stayed longer, but time was of the essence now in order that we reach Salou on time. The weather forecast was unpredictable, so we had to allow for bad weather possibly holding us up. Tarragona, like many of the places we were visiting along the coast of Spain, has a tremendous history. Founded in the 5th century BC, it was named Tarraco in Roman times. It was a shame we didn't have time to discover more, but we made ready for our sail the next morning heading for Salou.

Luckily, the winds were light and *Ipi 'n tombia* forged ahead at a fairly good speed. I enjoyed sitting at the tiller with one eye always on the compass, and the binoculars by my side to spot the dique (sea wall) as soon as we were near. We didn't have a pilot book for the Costa Dorada so it was more important than ever to look out for diques and landmarks such as the Torre Vella defence tower on the rugged coastline.

Late in the afternoon, Brian spotted the dique and we headed towards the marina. We passed strings of beautiful beaches interspersed with rocky coves and many holidaymakers sunning themselves. Taking in these new surroundings, we wound our way through the narrow entrance to the enclosed marina.

A marinera waved us into a space amongst several yachts and directed us to the Capitán's office to pay our dues - we would be staying five nights as my client was due to arrive in Salou the next day.

Having secured the yacht and paid, we discovered a restaurant on the quay, had dinner, and then ventured forth to explore the surrounding area. Although the beaches were beautiful, they were packed with tourists displaying sunburned bodies of all shapes and sizes. In the 1980's it was in vogue to go topless; in many cases not a pretty sight, so we weren't too impressed with the beach scene.

I phoned my Spanish friend who was going to meet up with my client and myself the next day at the marina. That evening, we climbed into our bunks early and woke refreshed next morning so that I was ready to abandon my yachting hat and replace it with my business hat. This was quite a difficult thing to do in such exotic surroundings, glorious weather, and very few clothes from which to choose. I chose some clean shorts, a cool top with sandals, and hoped I didn't look too casual for a business meeting.

No sooner had we finished breakfast in the cabin, than a loud knocking sounded on the forward hatch. A Spanish marinera was shouting *Ipi 'n tombia!* Wondering what on earth had happened, we popped our heads up through the hatch and asked him in Spanish what he wanted. He pointed towards the Club House across the quay and told us that my client had arrived and was waiting for me.

It was extremely unusual for me to do business with someone I had never met before. In fact, in the past I had made it a rule to meet my clients before I accompanied or met them in Spain to buy property. I always, always, made sure they were ready to buy with their cash available and didn't have a house to sell first, so this was my first encounter with an unqualified client. He had, however, been referred to me by a reputable Estate Agency in Kent, so I had decided they would have vetted him and not waste my time if he wasn't serious about buying. He certainly had a serious amount of money to spend on a warehouse for his goods, and a large property to live in, so I considered it was worth breaking our journey to help him to find what he was looking for.

I walked into the Club House and noticed a blonde Englishman standing at the bar drinking beer - I presumed it was him. I introduced myself and he told me a bit about himself and that he owned a luxury motor launch moored in Gibraltar which he sailed back and forth to Morocco (that should have issued a few warning bells, but didn't at the time!) He said that he and his wife, and two children had driven from England in their 4 x 4 but didn't have any accommodation booked for their stay in Salou. I knew there were several hotels nearby, so offered to take him and his family to find one to suit.

At the time I thought it rather odd that he had turned up with his family in a busy holiday resort in Spain without having booked accommodation. He was, however, a very personable chap and his wife and two children were polite nice people, so with my limited Spanish, I booked them into a hotel. I arranged to meet them that afternoon to show them properties once I had arranged a time with my Spanish colleague.

My colleague arrived promptly at 2pm on his motorbike and said he would drive ahead of the 4 x 4 so that we could all follow and he would show us a couple of houses and a warehouse (in this case, a converted bus depot). The first house was delightful - a large detached four-bed property standing in its own grounds with a large plot of land and a wonderful mistral's gallery inside. It was modernised throughout, with magnificent views and ideal for family living. They all agreed, including the children, that it would be an ideal place. After that, the other properties they saw were not in the running, so I felt good; it seemed that without any fuss whatsoever, a sale had been made. My colleague was delighted, proceeded to get on to his motorbike, and gestured for us to follow him again to the bus depot. Here again, it seemed the building was ideal for my client who said he was keen to wrap up the deal quickly.

I had sold many properties in various parts of the world over the years, but never such a quick and hassle-free sale... and a lucrative one at that.

My colleague said he would take over and deal with my client and his family from then on, leaving us to enjoy the rest of our stay on the yacht in Salou. As the sale had been so easy, I felt no qualms about leaving him to do the paperwork and handle it through to conclusion.

We enjoyed the remaining couple of days stay and I phoned my colleague prior to leaving to ensure everything was going through efficiently. He confirmed it was, so we carried on with our journey in fairly light seas.

At this point, I must mention that security in Spain in the 80's was excellent. Each time we checked in at a port or marina the Guardia Civil came aboard the yacht and filled in forms meticulously, wanting to know where we had come from and where we were going to, at the same time always checking our passports. They cut a dashing figure in their khaki/green uniforms with guns in their belts. We were to be grateful much later on that they were so efficient.

As we had no pilot book we were not quite sure whether our next stop would be Vinaròs or Amapola. When we spotted a bullring on the coast, we thought we were heading into Vinaròs, but it turned out to be Amapola. We found ourselves sailing into a pretty bay and decided we would find a quiet spot to drop anchor. In the distance, we could see a black vessel that looked very much like a pirate ship; we expected any moment to see pirates swinging off the rigging brandishing cutlasses, but it was soon apparent that it was deserted, as we could detect no movement at all. It was rather ghostly and would have been a good scene for a mystery movie. We were tempted to sail out to her to see if anyone was aboard or if anyone was in trouble, but decided against it as we could see weeds in the water beneath us that would mean we could run aground.

We dropped anchor and started to settle down for the night, getting our meal ready to eat in the cockpit, when out of nowhere, a deafening sound of pop music blasted through the hatch. "Oh no," we groaned as we realised we had anchored right next door to a disco - we had already experienced noise from several discos on our journey down the coast. Discos, and motorbikes like bees on steroids, were the bane of our life and many other yachtsmen told us they suffered the same problem.

We raised anchor and headed back around the bay looking for the entrance to the marina. We found a vacant mooring and went ashore to pay our dues. At least we would get a decent night's sleep - or so we thought. At about 7pm, fireworks started to appear in the sky and loud bangs echoed around us. Shouting and singing kicked off on in the local plaza and we thought we were no better off than if we had stayed anchored in the bay. That was until we heard the Catalan National Anthem being sung by a Spanish woman with a magnificent voice. The atmosphere was captivating as we listened to the anthem being sung with so much feeling whilst the sun went down - all was quiet now, except for the sound of her voice. All these years later, we have never forgotten the magic of that evening when. Instead of having to listen to the sound of a loud disco, we were honoured to be able to listen to singing with such beauty and reverence.

When we put our heads out of our cabin in the morning, we realised that it must be fiesta time in Amapola, for fireworks had started and children in Spanish costume were running around the streets followed by goats, dogs, and cats. Spanish ladies sat on chairs outside their pristine little houses, dressed in their finery chatting loudly to one another, whilst cyclists raced up and down the streets. This was in readiness for the first cycle race that was a very popular sport in Spain.

Nothing, however, prepared us for what was to come. A sudden silence pervaded, everyone stood to the side of the little cobbled street that ran through the village, then a mighty roar as about twenty bulls appeared at the top of the hill and ran madly towards the sea with several Spanish men following them shouting in glee.

We had just witnessed the famous 'Running of the Bulls' when the local Spanish men chased the bulls into the sea. This was the highlight of a week full of festivity. We realised that as we moved on down the coast, we would be witnessing various fiestas until the week was out, and looked forward to it very much. Sitting in the cockpit of our yacht was an ideal spot to enjoy all the activities that invariably took place near to the ports and marinas.

Full of festive spirit, we set off next morning for the next step on our exciting journey and agreed that we were enjoying every minute of the trip. We never knew what to expect in each fascinating place we stopped at.

We next happened upon Vinaròs, one of the major fishing ports along the Spanish coast. The town grew in the 16th and 17th centuries when navy yards and fortifications were built, and became very prosperous due to an involvement in shipbuilding and the wine trade. It suffered a strong decline in the early 20th century due to a plague of phylloxera that ruined the wine farming business. We discovered during our single night stay that Vinaròs was known for its tasty prawns.

It was obvious that the port was not a favourite spot for yachtsmen or any type of pleasure craft, as we couldn't find a place to tie up for a long time when we entered the dique. Eventually, some fishermen spotted us along the bank, waved us towards the town wall, and helped us to tie up against their fishing boats. One of the fishermen was the image of Charles Bronson - even his mannerisms. Perhaps it was Charles Bronson? He never spoke a word, so there was no proof that he was Spanish!

We decided to have an early night in readiness to discover the town next morning. We could hear the familiar sound of fireworks in the distance so assumed that the festivities were taking place here as well as in Amapola.

The next morning, the sun shone down on us as we ate our breakfast in the cockpit with the fishermen looking on as if we were from outer space. It was evident that they didn't often get visiting yachtsmen into their harbour. They were a friendly lot though, and insisted on giving us some fish. Unfortunately, we didn't know how to gut it, so with much gesticulating, one of them went off and gutted it for us ready for cooking.

The walk into town only took about ten minutes and we took our water can with us to fill up with some fresh water. We often frequented the village town pumps when ashore to make sure we had the pure water fresh from the mountains. We realised that we were running short of money, so before visiting the town water pump, we looked around for a bank. We asked an elderly Spanish man who was sitting on a bench smoking a pipe if he knew of a nearby bank. He pointed up a narrow street and told us it was at the end, however, when we arrived we found the doors were locked even though we could see a man behind the counter through the window of the door. We were getting worried as we needed more pesetas to buy provisions and diesel so we knocked on the door, not expecting him to answer, as the bank was obviously closed for the fiesta. We were just about to walk away wondering what on earth we were going to do when the door opened and a cheery small Spanish man with jet black hair smoothed back from his forehead greeted us and asked us what we wanted. I explained in Spanish that we had no money at all, that we were on a yacht, and didn't know how we were to get provisions. I gave him my most charming smile that generally did the trick with Spanish men, and true to form, he gestured to us to enter the bank and asked how much we wanted. To my dismay, I then realised I hadn't brought my passport with me for identification - all banks asked for this in Spain. I did have my driving licence with me, so I presented it to him and he took it and wrote a number down on a piece of paper and gave us the money we wanted. We were so grateful and thanked him profusely for serving us during fiesta; he was quite cheerful about it and told us that we must not miss the very important annual cycling race that was soon to start in the square.

After filling up our water can, we looked around for a place to buy coffee and spotted a little café in the town square where we could sit on the pavement and watch the preparation for that morning's festivities. All the streets were closed off and there was an official-looking Spaniard dressed in a very smart uniform standing in the middle of the road. He was unsuccessfully trying to organise the traffic, since although the streets were closed, the cars kept coming.

The idea was that all the streets should be free of cars to give the cyclists free access, but it just wasn't happening - cars continued to wind their way through the streets just as the race was about to start.

Eventually, a local policeman arrived complete with truncheon and a whistle. With much shouting and gesticulating, he marked a spot in the middle of the road with his foot and instructed the official who was the organiser of the race to stand there. Motorists were thus unable to pass him to go up the street where the cycling race was to take place - a human barrier!

After much shouting and whistling, the drivers eventually got the picture and started to go the other way around, which solved the problem. This was until the organiser, to our amusement, became distracted by a pretty young girl on a moped who pleaded with him that it was of the utmost importance that she drive through the route the cyclists were due to take.

Not able to resist a pretty face, the official waved her through. This opened the floodgates and cars and mopeds appeared from all directions and followed her. Luckily, the policeman who had told the official not to let any cars through had disappeared, otherwise there would have been further delays.

The result, however, was that the cyclists at the start of the race had to weave their way through oncoming cars, mopeds, ox carts, and every other vehicle imaginable - it was more like an obstacle race.

We drank our coffee and thought to ourselves that this is what we like about Spain. The Spanish people are a delight to observe, they take life as it comes and do not necessarily stick to any rules.

We remember Vinaròs to this day as being the port of helpful, friendly fishermen, and the famous cycle race.

We weren't so sure about the fishermen next morning though; when we asked about the weather forecast, they told us very calm seas. But when we were out in the open sea, force 5-6 and rough seas greeted us!

Chapter 13

Costa del Azahar. Luckily, the wind was in our direction so we enjoyed an exhilarating sail to our next destination - Peñíscola. In those days, it was just a tiny port with not many fishermen, but tourism was flourishing.

We weaved our way into the harbour under motor, heading towards a few rather doubtful looking boats tied up against a wall, and managed to squeeze in between two of them. Although the mooring appeared rather scruffy, when we had settled down and tied up, we were impressed with the beautiful beaches and surrounding area that we could see over the rocky wall. A friendly Spanish man by the name of Obi, who lived on his yacht all year round earning his living by painting fairground equipment, came by to see us and told us something of the history of Peñíscola.

He said it was often called the Gibraltar of Valencia and pointed out to us that there was a lighthouse and castle built on a rocky headland about 220 feet high that joined the mainland by a narrow strip of land. The castle was originally built by the Knights Templar between 1294 and 1307. He said that the castle had been restored and improved with new walls added in 1960 and was now a famous tourist attraction. Obi was a mine of information and seemed to know everything there was to know about Peñíscola, a name derived from the Latin word, peninsula.

We decided we would spend some time discovering Peñíscola, as we needed to replace the impellor on our water pump, and had to find a place that would have one - we knew this would be no mean feat.

We were accustomed to paying mooring fees wherever we stopped, but Obi told us that the reason he moored there was because it was not necessary to pay. We could understand why; there was no water or electricity available, we would manage with our gas stove for cooking, and rely on getting water from the town square and gas from the nearest ferretería (hardware store).

During the night, one of the boats left, leaving an empty space. This was soon occupied by a motorboat that moored next to us with much shouting and cheering going on by the occupants who seemed to be Spanish fishermen.

Needless to say, we didn't get much sleep, and next morning we were rudely awakened by a loudspeaker blaring out across the water announcing, "Ali, Ali, Ali!" We thought there was some terrible emergency, so rushed up into the cockpit in our nightclothes to find Obi sitting in his cockpit eating his breakfast.

"No problema," he said. "That is the pleasure craft calling to tourists to go aboard for a day trip round the bay. You will hear that two or three times a day, but thankfully not at night, unless they decide to do a moonlight trip."

We could see that staying in Peñíscola was going to be a noisy, albeit interesting sojourn. Eventually *Ali Ali* seemed to have captured enough tourists to set out on her mystery trip round the bay, so we settled down to breakfast in the cockpit, and afterwards, took a leisurely stroll to the nearest beach.

Memories of our stay in Port Lligat on the Costa Brava came rushing back to us immediately - everyone on the beach was naked. These naturist beaches were scattered all along the coast of Spain. The French and Spanish liked more than to discard their clothes and strut around naked on the beach. But to our prudish minds, we couldn't see the point, as most of the bodies were not a pretty sight.

We decided not to stay on the beach, opting to visit the castle on the hill instead - it was worth the visit. It was just like a typical Spanish village. Tiny shops and steep steps led to pristine terraced houses with ladies dressed in black sitting outside on chairs or religiously scrubbing the part of the street in front of their homes. They all greeted us cheerily. Window boxes overflowed with colourful flowers and donkeys clattered down the streets followed by wizened men encouraging them to keep going with sticks. Even though there were many tourists around, it didn't spoil the relaxed, leisurely atmosphere. We visited the castle many times before we left Peñíscola.

We found the town water pump after guidance from our newly found friend, Obi, and visited the ferretería where we got a gas container. It seemed, however, that there was nowhere we could buy a new impellor for our water pump. Obi told us to try La Rapita, which wasn't far away, so we found the local bus stop and waited half an hour until the bus arrived. We wandered around for about an hour before we found a tumble down garage in one of the small side streets - this sounded like the place Obi had described to us. To our amazement, a Spaniard who was wearing greasy overalls and mending some sort of engine, told us he could help us but that we would have to order it and go back in a week's time.

We hadn't planned to stay in Peñíscola for so long, particularly as there was no electricity or water readily available. But at least it was free, and the area was a delight, so it was another two weeks before we would continue on our travels.

The evening before we were ready to leave, several yachts entered the harbour seeking moorings. Since there were none available, two yachts rafted up next to us. A little later, a large luxury yacht came in named *Lisa*. With much shouting and waving, the German skipper, dressed in immaculate white trousers, black blazer with a gold anchor on the pocket and peaked cap, motored towards us hoping to raft up against a Swiss yacht who in turn was rafted up against us. It was, however, obvious that the skipper had little or no knowledge at all of handling a boat. He tried to secure his springs (bow and aft ropes) first, and then threw a warp wildly to anyone who happened to be there. This immediately dropped into the water, but Brian and the Swiss yachtsman eventually managed to help tie him alongside the Swiss man's yacht.

The motorboat looked completely out of place amongst all the sailing yachts. Emerging from the luxurious cabin, the skipper's girlfriend dressed in a flimsy white dress and high heels. She looked disdainfully at us yachties whilst she sat in the luxurious aft deck painting her nails.

Maybe *Lisa*'s skipper and his girlfriend couldn't speak any English, or maybe they were just unfriendly, since they made no attempt to speak to ourselves, Obi, or the Swiss yachtsman rafted up next to us.

Next morning at about 6am, we were rudely awakened with our yacht shuddering wildly; when we looked out of our cabin, we saw the German skipper starting to rev up his engines in readiness to leave. He was about to cast off, not realising that if he did so, it would leave us adrift. We tried to explain to him that you couldn't just up and go when you were rafted up with other boats, but he took no notice. He threw the ropes into the water and headed off, leaving the Swiss chap's yacht floating out towards the harbour entrance. Unfortunately, the Swiss chap was ashore at the time, so when he realised what was happening, he had to take a mighty leap from the quayside in order to get aboard and gain control. He nearly fell into the water. We were all glad to see the German and his girlfriend leave; they had been the most unpleasant characters we had encountered so far on our journey.

We collected our impellor at La Rapita and it was now fitted to our water pump, so we decided to say goodbye to our good friend, Obi, and head out to sea. This time, our destination was the Costa Blanca, where Dénia would be our first port of call.

We had read that several times a year the city of Dénia was full of festivities. In March, a popular bonfire festival is celebrated when huge papier-mâché statues, called fallas are set up throughout the town and then set alight. The term 'fallas' refers to both the celebration and the sculptures created for it. We had already seen the running of the bulls in Amapola so were not concerned about missing this rather disconcerting activity, which would have taken place before our arrival.

We passed by the vast port of Valencia, the largest on the Mediterranean coast. During the 1980's, Valencia was mainly an industrial city, but rapid development in the mid-90's expanded its cultural and tourism possibilities. Valencia is famous for the Las Fallas traditional celebration honouring Saint Joseph and for the popular dish - Paella Valenciana - containing rice with fish or chicken.

Little did we know that, in the future, we would return to enter the port in a luxurious motorboat (complete with a helicopter on deck). This would be in the role of translator and crewman. As a translator, however, I learned to my dismay that there were two official languages - Valencian and Castilian Spanish. I was able to cope with Castilian but was stumped when it came to Valencian!

The wind was 4 - 5 with a moderate sea, so we made good headway towards Dénia in the province of Alicante on the Costa Blanca. Here again we were to discover that the city had a great and interesting history.

Chapter 14

Costa Blanca. We tried to be in safe harbour by 4pm in the afternoon when the dreaded Mistral was to most likely to blow up. Also, the fishermen often returned to their port between 4pm and 5pm in the afternoon and would rush in towards the port in large groups. This caused a huge wash, so any yacht within reach could be in for a rough ride.

So it was 4pm when we sailed into the harbour at Dénia. We noticed a couple of yachts were anchored in the harbour, which would save us having to pay mooring fees, and it looked as though it could be a very pleasant anchorage. We dropped anchor into the crystal clear water, watching it rest on the seabed and making firm. We sat in the cockpit to take in our surroundings.

We looked up to see a fortress overlooking the harbour and the city; we made a note to visit and find out about its history. We could hear fireworks in the distance and much laughter and Spanish Flamenco. July and August were certainly the months of festivities along the coast of Spain.

We lifted our *Bombard* dinghy into the water and made fast the *Evinrude* outboard in readiness to motor ashore to top up with supplies and discover the town. As we were doing so, a rather strange sight caught our eye. A yacht with what appeared to be two huge Perspex globes hanging from the side. We couldn't figure out what they were, but the next day the owner of the boat rowed over to us and we invited him aboard. He was from Wales, had come across the Bay of Biscay to the Mediterranean, and was experimenting with his invention. The theory was apparently that if the yacht got into trouble - or indeed the skipper got into trouble - he could exit the yacht and climb into the Perspex globe for safety. Brian and I decided secretly that we would rather be cast out to sea than spend any time rolling around in a Perspex ball! Nevertheless, we didn't hurt his feelings by telling him so, and wished him luck with his experiment.

To our delight, the famous Moors & Christians festival was due to take place in the town square, and we had arrived just in time to see it in all its splendour. It proved to be the most impressive festival we had witnessed during our trip. Crowds lined the streets with little children dressed in traditional costumes, the girls swirling their colourful dresses proudly, and the boys strutting around in their black long trousers with cummerbund, spotless white shirts, bow ties and the traditional matador hat resting jauntily on their heads.

There was a hush as the first three elephants appeared dressed in magnificent finery with their masters sitting proudly on their backs and waving to the crowds. Cheers then sounded out as the elephants slowly trundled down the street, followed by the famous horses of the Camargue, their riders dressed in Spanish style, proudly waving, with the horses rearing up and dancing round in circles.

Flamenco dancers followed in colourful dresses, lovingly sewn by doting mothers and grandmothers in readiness for this very special fiesta. Flamenco music started to play and the crowds broke free to dance and sing in the square. The atmosphere was electric and when Brian and I joined in the dancing, we were welcomed with glee by the friendly local people.

The festivities went on well into the night and, exhausted, we finally rowed across to our yacht in the dinghy, climbed aboard, and collapsed in our berths without any thought of an evening meal.

The next morning, we visited the fortress that stood in the middle of the town. It turned out to be a partial ruin and we learned that there was evidence of human habitation in the area since prehistoric times with significant Iberian ruins on the hillsides nearby. The Moors originally built the fortress, and the French, who occupied the city for four years during the War of the Spanish Succession, rebuilt it in the early 19th century. A community of English raisin traders lived in Dénia from 1800 until the time of the Spanish Civil war in the late 1930s.

Today, it is not possible to anchor in Dénia as we did. A marina has been constructed with purpose-built berths, so perhaps the tranquillity we enjoyed has disappeared forever.

The weather forecast was good for the next morning, so we made preparations to proceed on our journey, this time heading for Moraira, a small coastal town lying 80 km north of the city of Alicante and 100 km south of Valencia. It was a glorious morning with the sun shining down from a cloudless sky. I sat in the cockpit, guiding the yacht through the tranquil sea, keeping an eye on the compass. Brian perched himself on the pulpit looking for the dique through binoculars.

Finally, we spotted an entrance to a little bay and dropped anchor in pure crystal water. There were no other yachts in the bay and it was again, as if paradise found. There was no doubt that this was the delightful fishing village of Moraira, and still unspoiled by tourism. We could see tiny fincas and casas on the undulating coastline but no sign of life anywhere. We spotted large vineyards in the distance and realised that Moraira must be a wine growing area. Later, a fisherman came in with the fleet that afternoon, and explained that Moraira was famous for the growing of Muscatel grapes for wine making.

It was midday with the sun blazing down, so we donned our swimsuits and launched the dingy. We had found it impossible to climb on and off the yacht even with our ladders, so we scrambled on to the dinghy first, before jumping into the clear water to swim. After we had cooled off, we took a cruise around the area in the dinghy and could see that here there was no sign of high-rise buildings; the tiny fincas and hamlets blended into the countryside, retaining the village atmosphere of its heritage. A law had been passed in the area to protect the abundant pine trees and to limit the height of buildings, and thus Moraira had been saved from the horrors of tourism.

That evening, we abandoned our *Evinrude* engine and rowed ashore, not wishing to spoil the tranquillity of the area. We went in search of a something to eat as we felt we were bound to fine an authentic Spanish restaurant in such a lovely village. It did not take us long; we discovered three fantastic restaurants with very appealing menus. The one we chose served exquisite food, inevitably with muscatel wine, and excellent service.

We hope Moraira has managed to escape mass tourism - it was one of the most beautiful fishing villages we visited during our adventure.

The next morning, another visiting yacht sailed in and dropped anchor not far away from us, but we didn't have time to make their acquaintance. We were moving on again, but we waved to them - wishing them a happy stay as sailed out of the bay and into a choppy sea.

The town of Calpe was on our route, but we were not too keen on stopping there as we had been told that a lot of yachting people named 'dead beats' were anchored there in a group. We didn't know whether to feel sorry or annoyed with the group who, in those days, gave the yachting fraternity a bad name. In the 80's, it was in vogue to sell up and sail and many books were written about this dream. In many cases, the dream sadly became a nightmare. Many yachtsmen did not realise how costly it could be to live aboard a yacht, maintain it, and be ready to pay costly mooring fees at marinas or anchorages. As a result, sailors who ran out of money inevitably looked for areas where they could moor their boats free or at a very low price and they formed groups in various areas such as Calpe along the coast. We encountered quite a few people who had not done their homework before setting out from their homeland; although they had paid for their boat, they had invariably sold their house, leaving them little choice other than to live aboard permanently as their remaining funds dwindled.

We passed the famous Rock of Ifach and were sorry that we couldn't explore the town and learn of the history. We'd heard that there were many Iberian, Roman, and Arab archaeological sites in the town, including the ruins of Los Baños de la Reina (the Queen's baths).

Ipi 'n tombia coasted through the choppy sea at quite a pace, but the wind was not in the right direction, so we started up the engine to ensure we reached our next destination in good time. This was to avoid the dreaded *Afternoon Hate*, as we called, it at 4pm - a time when the wind usually blew at its strongest, and the fishing fleets rushed into port.

We were heading for Alicante, an impressive city with a tremendous history. But in view of the choppy seas and the wind blowing in the wrong direction, we decided to see if we could anchor in Altea, which is protected on the north by the bluffs of the Sierra Bernia, creating a lovely, almost tropical, climate. This was confirmed when we sailed into the wide bay of Altea and dropped anchor in front of a group of cruising yachts. We could see beautiful beaches and exotic palm trees lining the seafront esplanade.

For the third time on our journey, we slipped anchor and nearly bumped into the yacht in front of us. Luckily, an English chap popped his head over the stern and fended us off with his boat hook. We apologised profusely and made good the anchor further away from him. He stopped by in his dinghy on the way to the beach to do some shopping and asked us if he could get us any supplies, but we told him we were going ashore to explore, and invited him aboard for drinks later that evening. He was a single handed sailor in a 30' *Elizabethan* yacht similar in design to our *Tyler Tufglass* 33'.

After he had left, we lowered ourselves down into the dinghy, only to find that our engine refused to spark into life. It just spluttered and died, so we took up the oars and rowed to the beach.

We strolled along the pretty promenade, resplendent with its tropical flowers and palm trees. We found our way to the old town, a maze of cobbled, narrow, and crooked streets, with whitewashed terraced houses. Black-clad ladies sat outside on straight backed chairs or scrubbing the pavement. They all greeted us as we passed by. Our Spanish had progressed quite well by now, so we could have a limited conversation with them, which pleased them very much.

Elderly farmers sat in the local tapas bar with their donkeys outside as they enjoyed their morning coffee, cognac, and iced water. We learned long ago, that the bars in Spanish villages were purely the domain of the man - women were not allowed! On the floor beneath the bar at each of these sacred places was cigarette ash and sawdust (the sign of a used bar). The rest of the bar area was spotless, including the restrooms.

We found a small shop - one of the whitewashed houses converted into a grocery store - with everything from matches to wine crammed into every nook and cranny. We were greeted with great enthusiasm by the proprietor who was most helpful and very proud that he could let us have freshly baked bread - baked that morning by his wife.

We sauntered out of the shop with our shopping trolley full and noticed a building with picturesque blue and white domes, tiled with glazed ceramics. We were fascinated, so, despite our heavy shopping, went to discover what the building was and were surprised to find that it was a church: La Mare de Déu del Consol (Our Lady of Solace). It wasn't a conventional design for a church but was spectacular and no doubt a great tourist attraction.

It seemed that Altea was a mix of old and new; tourism was gradually finding its way to the beautiful tropical beaches and the grand old town.

We were feeling very thirsty as we headed back towards our dinghy that hopefully awaited us in its storage position: upside down with the oars inside on the beach. We spotted a little beachside bar, sat outside, and ordered two of the local beers. I wasn't a beer drinker, but during the voyage, the weather was so warm, I found I could drink beer as long as it was ice cold. We were very impressed to see when the waiter brought our beer that the beer glasses were frosted inside and out, making the beer even more refreshing.

Our dinghy was safely where we left it, so we made our way back to the yacht, finding it difficult to row with our heavy shopping weighing the dinghy down. The conditions starting to blow up as the 4pm *Afternoon Hate* began to make its presence felt.

Luckily, our newfound English friend had spotted us and helped us pull alongside the side of our yacht and load our shopping aboard. He also offered to help Brian mend our engine the next morning whilst I rowed myself ashore to get my hair cut as I had noticed a Peluquería, a hairdressers, near the beach.

We spent the rest of the day lazing on the beach and enjoying a swim in the now calm sea. There were many tourists on the beaches - not surprising as the weather in Altea felt almost tropical.

With a fine weather forecast, we rose from our bunks at 8am next morning and waved goodbye to our friend who was heading in the opposite direction on his way back to the UK.

Alicante, the historic Mediterranean port, was to be our next stop. We'd heard a lot about it from friends we had known at the Essex Marina Yacht Club near Burnham on Crouch, Essex. They had sailed their 30' yacht from the marina to Alicante together with their three children, and had anchored there for a year.

As we entered the harbour, we could see several boats tied against the quay, which in those days was right next to the main road leading into the town. We decided it would be better to drop anchor rather than be tied to the quay - people were walking up and down right next to the boats, and traffic from the main road might be noisy.

As soon as we had dropped anchor, we took the dinghy and went ashore to discover the port area; it was very convenient as we were almost in the main town. We found ourselves walking along the esplanade adjacent to the quay where there were interesting looking little stalls, cafes and restaurants. In the 80's, the port area was not as sophisticated as it is today. Today, there is a newly built area of the marina with pubs, bars, and cinemas that stay open until the early hours.

After stocking up with supplies in a supermarket (some items of which we hadn't seen in a long time), we headed back to the yacht and decided to rest up until the next day when we planned to explore the more of the town and surrounding areas.

Another yacht had entered the harbour whilst we had been away and dropped anchor just behind us. They were French and didn't speak any English, but with my smattering of French that I learned in my College days, we managed to greet one another and say a few words.

The following morning, we headed for the Santa Barbara Castle that was perched on top of Mount Benacantil overlooking the sea. We picked up a leaflet on its history and read that it was one of Spain's largest medieval fortresses. The views of the city were spectacular. Later, whilst walking along the palm-lined promenade of Postiguet beach, we looked up and we could see the Cara del Moro or Moor's Head that is an unusual outcrop in the shape of a human face.

After lunch at a delightful tapas bar, we headed for the Santa Cruz quarter of the old town. The locals know this quarter as El Barrio. It is a fascinating area, steeped in history and home to the majority of the city's monuments. We were breathless when we reached the quarter as it is situated in the highest part, but mercifully, it was free of traffic. When we reached the top, the views were spectacular so it was well worth the hike.

We also located the Las Agustinas Convent in the old quarter. It was built in the eighteenth century to house Jesuits and we were much impressed when we saw the image of the Virgen de la Soledad - the focal point of the oldest of Alicante's Holy week celebrations.

Exhausted after our interesting day out in Alicante, we headed back to pick up our dinghy from the quay. Thanks to our friend at Altea who helped to mend our *Evinrude* outboard motor, we motored back to the yacht, climbed aboard and collapsed on our bunks - falling asleep without even thinking about an evening meal.

The next morning, the weather was still very hot, so we put our swimming costumes on and dived into the water. Despite the harbour being next to the main road, in those days it was not a very busy, so the sea remained unpolluted.

Feeling refreshed, we prepared to set off in calm seas to our next port of call, which would be Torrevieja.

Torrevieja (meaning Old Tower) is situated approximately thirty miles south of the city of Alicante on the Costa Blanca. Since our traumatic trip across the Gulf of Lion, our Bukh engine had behaved itself and reassuringly chugged along without faltering; assisting our sails as there was not a breath of air. When running the engine continuously, we always had to keep an eye on the amount of diesel in the tank, as it could be disastrous to run out and not be able to motor when there was no wind. We also rigged up an overhead cover to shade us from the sun and to avoid sunburn. This, of course, had to be taken down if the wind picked up.

Torrevieja was originally a salt-mining and fishing village located between the sea and two large salt lakes (Las Salinas).

We spotted the entrance to a small harbour and dropped anchor. Here, like many of the anchorages, the water was beautifully clear and we watched as the anchor unfurled to the bottom and took hold. We stripped off our shorts and tops and dived into the water to cool off as the sun was beating down mercilessly.

We were the only yacht anchored in the harbour and we swam for a while before climbing aboard for lunch in the cockpit. As we had topped up with quite a few provisions in Alicante, there was no immediate need to go ashore for shopping, so we decided to leave exploring the town until the next day and enjoy a leisurely afternoon enjoying the peace and glorious sunshine.

During the summer months, there were many festivities throughout Spain. Torrevieja, however, was one exception. Although the day of the Virgin del Carmen on July 16th was celebrated with a day off, there were not as many events taking place as other places we had visited. We didn't know it at the time, but we were to witness the fantastic spectacle of the Virgin del Carmen when we moored at a small fishing harbour in

Caleta de Vélez, later on our journey.

Despite being quieter in terms of fiestas, we discovered the Fiesta de música, a music festival which was in full swing with a variety of musicians performing - local bands, orchestras, soloists and choral societies. We also came across the street market on the promenade by the port. Here, all sorts of bargains could be had, such as clothing, fruit, vegetables, leather, shoes, handbags, bedding, and curtains.

Our stay in Torrevieja was just for one night and we prepared to move to Mar Menor further down the coast. Brian had been very keen on reaching Mar Menor, a salty lagoon in the south eastern autonomous community of Murcia, as he had visions of anchoring in calm waters for a couple of weeks and possibly leaving the yacht there when we returned to England for the winter.

We set out the next morning full of anticipation and thoughts of settling in one place for a while. Our hopes were soon dashed as the weather took a turn for the worse; halfway through our journey, a nasty storm blew up and we had difficulty in finding our way into the lagoon.

We found ourselves in the middle of what appeared to be a number of lakes with little islands dotted around. We tried to shelter on the lee of an island but the wind was even too forceful there. Several windsurfers were in trouble, as they had not anticipated there would be such a storm. Ahead of us, a few motorboats were able to manoeuvre despite the storm, so we assumed they would go to the aid of the windsurfers. To our disgust, however, they left them in distress and headed back to their moorings.

Brian became enveloped in the mainsail as he attempted to get in down in the storm - it came down in a heap on top of him. In the meantime, I was trying to steer *Ipi 'n tombia* in the direction of the two windsurfers who were shouting and waving to us for help. Eventually, we reached one of them, dragged him aboard, and managed to tie his board and sail on to the back of the boat, despite the wind tugging it in every direction. He was exhausted, but worried about his friend who was still struggling against the unabating might of the wind. We turned around and motored towards him, ever conscious that if a gust of wind overpowered us, we could end up running him down. I was in charge at the helm and prayed I was getting it right. Brian and the young fellow we had rescued were leaning over the pushpit at the stern with their arms out in order to grab him.

With a huge struggle, they managed to help him aboard and tie his windsurfing equipment on the back of the yacht. Brian took over the tiller whilst I went below to get two blankets, as they were both shivering - not so much with the cold, but with fright.

We had no idea where we were; the two windsurfers spoke no English, and in any case, were too traumatised to speak. The wind was strengthening, rather than dying down, but in the distance, we spotted some bungalows on the bank and headed towards them. Through a bit of luck, we saw a small private mooring - possibly belonging to one of the houses - and the owner must have been away or no longer mooring his boat there.

One of the occupants of the houses came out to the mooring when he spotted our dilemma; we threw a line to him and he tied us on temporarily. We were extremely grateful to him, as after all the drama, we too were now beginning to feel fatigued.

The windsurfers had recovered and thanked us profusely for helping them. They remarked in Spanish about the way the motorboats had left them - possibly to drown. It would have been much easier for a motorboat to carry out the rescue, but we were just thankful that we had been able to help them.

They headed off after securing their windsurfing gear near the quay and we decided to settle down for the night, hoping the storm would pass by morning.

It had taken us by surprise and, as was often the case in the Mediterranean at the time, the weather forecast had been entirely wrong, predicting light winds. We were beginning to wonder if this was the sort of weather which occurred frequently in Mar Menor, and if so, our plan to stay there for any length of time was no longer on the agenda.

After a bumpy night, with the yacht leaping around and making weird noises with the fenders scraping against the quay, we rose at 8am to find the storm had abated. The sky was clear and the inland lakes looked calm. It was a very different scene to the one we'd encountered on our arrival.

We were having breakfast in the cockpit, when the occupant of the house who had helped us tie up during the storm, came over. He wanted to see if he could help us in any way - we told him we would be looking for a marina in order to stay in Mar Menor for a while. He told us that we were now at a small urbanisation named Mar de Cristal that comprised some very pretty houses with well-kept gardens. Apparently, people of all nationalities had bought properties there, some with moorings. The owner of the mooring we were tied up to was presently out sailing, so we had been very fortunate to come across it empty, otherwise, it would have been extremely difficult in the storm to find anywhere else.

He provided directions to a marina called Thomas Mastrae, so when we had finished breakfast, we prepared the yacht and set off under motor. We'd heard that this was a sporting area with yachting, golf, tennis, and fine restaurants. We were disappointed, however, when we eventually arrived at Thomas Mastrae to find that the marina looked as if it was only half completed and had a feeling of neglect about it. Brian was particularly disappointed, as he had read about the Mar Menor before leaving England and it had been his aim to moor there permanently. He felt it would be a safe haven to leave the yacht when we returned to England, but looking around us, that was not going to be the case.

We had a meal in a rather mediocre restaurant situated just opposite the marina and expressed our disappointment to an English couple who had moored their yacht beside us. They said they were heading for Gibraltar, but told us of a brand new marina on the Costa del Sol with a thousand moorings. It offered good rates for wintering - namely Almerimar, it was situated not far from Almería. Unbeknown to us at the time, this was to be our second home for many years to come and still is.

Chapter 15

We left Mar Menor in much calmer waters than when we had arrived and were not sorry to leave and be on our way. Brian was feeling queasy after the previous night's meal, so we decided we would stop at the nearest reasonable looking marina or fishing port, which turned out to be Mazarrón on the lesser-known coast of Costa Calida.

The entrance to the small marina proved tricky to negotiate as it was enclosed by rocks on either side. I managed to guide us through as by now, Brian was almost past caring with stomach cramps - I had to find a place to tie up. Murphy's Law, there was not one place available that wasn't occupied by either a yacht or a motorboat and I thought we would have to raft up. Luckily, a Spanish yachtsman was standing on the pontoons and waved me towards a narrow space that was available; at the same time as steering the yacht in, I managed to throw the warps to him and he tied us up. I thanked him and told him that I was a single handed at present since my husband was ill - he sympathised and asked if he could help in any way. He told me that the mooring was only available for just one night as it belonged to his friend who would be back first thing in the morning. Considering Brian's state, this was bad news, but at least we could rest up for a while before heading off the next morning.

I foraged in the First Aid box and found some Imodium. It did the trick - he began to feel better immediately and managed to eat a bowl of chicken soup we had stashed away in our food locker. Luck, however, was not with us, and no sooner had we sat down to eat, than huge mosquitoes invaded the cabin. They were unlike any we had come across on our travels before - even biting us through our clothes. Unfortunately, we didn't have the marvellous plug-in mosquito deterrent one can buy in the chandleries these days. All we had was some ointment that we rubbed into all the exposed parts of our bodies and squirted spray around. We made fast mosquitoes nets on the forward and cabin hatches and bedded down for the night.

Next morning, we were awakened at 7am by knocking on the bow of the yacht - it was the Spanish man who we had met the previous day. He informed us that his friend was now back and drifting about in the marina, waiting for his mooring. Thankfully, Brian was feeling better, though both of us were scratching huge mosquito bites on our arms and legs. We fired up the engine and made ready to leave the mooring, waving to our Spanish friend as we made our way through the hazardous entrance towards the sea. A strong wind was blowing and it took the strength of two of us to handle the tiller, keeping away from the rocks on either side, as we were caught in a huge swell. We were very relieved when we had exited the marina as we could have suffered a capsize in the conditions that thankfully subsided when we reached the open sea. We were then able put up the sails to steady the yacht. The beauty of a sailing yacht is that in bad weather, the sails stabilise the motion and make for an easier passage. Also, there is not such a great reliance on the engine and therefore failures can usually be handled using the sails and not seeking assistance from the coastguard or other vessels. These advantages are not extended to some forms of leisure motorboats; depending on the design, the motion in rough weather can be terrible, and engine failures, potentially dangerous.

Cheered by the brilliant sunshine, whilst trying not to scratch our mosquito bites, which by now were huge red bumps on our arms and legs, we enjoyed a brisk sail towards our next destination, Águilas.

Brian, balancing on the pulpit, spotted a marina in the distance and we hoped there would be room there for us to stay at least a couple of nights to recover from our uncomfortable hasty stop at Mazarrón.

We entered the seaport of Águilas situated in the province of Murcia (Costa Calida) and could see some beautiful white sandy beaches with people sunbathing and swimming in the sea. On our approach, we had to be very careful that there was no-one swimming too close to the yacht. Águilas is built on the side of a small peninsula between two bays - the Puerto Poniente and the Puerto Levante.

We dropped anchor in a delightful secluded spot, donned our swimsuits, and dived into the sea to cool off before lunch. Our supplies had been depleted somewhat because of our stay at Mazarrón where we were unable to stock up, so Brian decided to lower the *Bombard* dinghy and row over to the shore where we could see some shops. I had forgotten that he spoke no Spanish at all, so wasn't surprised when he told me that he had to flap his arms up and down to make the shopkeeper know that he wanted eggs. The language exercises continued. Later that evening, a French yacht anchored nearby and they too swam in the sea and waved to us; I tried to converse with them in French with limited success.

We took off in the dinghy again and left it ashore whilst we went to discover the town. During the second half of the 19th century, a vast British colony arrived and we could almost feel the British presence as we looked around the various buildings, including an old house of an English merchant and a British cemetery.

After the dodgy meal at Mar Menor, we were tending to eat more on the yacht as we had vowed to be a bit more discerning about the restaurants we chose from now on. We rustled up some salad and fruit and nursing our mosquito bites, took to our bunks at about 10pm, only to be kept awake all night by the incessant howling of dogs from the town. This was accompanied by the most dreadful odour that seeped into every nook and cranny of the yacht.

By morning, we felt positively nauseous and realised that during the night, the town's sewage had been poured into the sea. We were even more amazed to see the French couple, seemingly unaware of the bad smell, swimming amongst the sewage.

Despite the beauty of the area, we decided not stay any longer in Águilas and swiftly headed out to sea.

After receiving the recommendation from the people who had moored next to us at Mar Menor, we decided our route would eventually take us to the new marina which had just been built at Almerimar. Here we would leave our yacht over the winter months, as we needed to return to the UK and our long neglected house on Canvey Island. The local estate agents had rented out the property to a pop group, so we were hoping they weren't practicing their music in the house or garden and disturbing our neighbours.

We checked the pilot book and planned a stop at Garrucha - a municipality of Almería province. After Garrucha, the pilot informed us to look for a distinctive landmark: three high-rise blocks of apartments that would guide us into the marina of Almerimar.

Garrucha turned out to be an industrial port with cement works just opposite the half-finished pontoons where we eventually tied up. We went ashore to look for supplies, setting off along the pontoon, only to discover it came to a sudden end with a big drop into the water. We only just managed to prevent ourselves falling in, complete with shopping trolley.

Everywhere was horribly dusty and we didn't like the look of the place at all. The cement works was repeatedly belching out huge clouds of dust and everywhere was covered in white cement. Nevertheless, we needed supplies, so put the dinghy over the side, and motored ashore. Outside the half-finished marina, Garrucha did look a little better. The harbour is defended by an ancient castle and there proved to be many seafront bars and restaurants serving locally produced food from the farms and surrounding area.

We stocked up with food, and luckily, we had enough diesel and water to take us all the way to Almerimar; we would suffer one night on the yacht in Garrucha and head off for the next stop along the way, San José, next morning.

When we returned the yacht we found another rafted up next to us, and to our dismay, a woman in her mid twenties came up on deck crying. She was English, so we asked her what her problem was; she told us that she was on honeymoon with her husband and they had set out from England to sail to the Caribbean. Looking at the yacht, which was much smaller than ours was, we thought that it was very ambitious. She said they had been held up - sheltering behind the Cabo de Gata headland from storms for over a week with little food or water. Her husband had eventually found his way ashore to try to find water, but we knew there was nowhere he could fill up his tank with water at Garrucha.

We felt very sorry for them, and since we had a full tank of water and endless bottles of fresh drinking water below our bunks, we handed her several bottles that would at least get them to where they were going.

Her husband turned up empty handed as we were talking to her and they had a terrible row, as he had not managed to find food or water. I raided my cupboards and gave them tins of beans, potatoes, tomatoes and anything else I could find which would hopefully sustain them until they reached a marina where they could stock up for themselves.

Unfortunately, they were typical of many people we met on our journey who had set out full of dreams but not properly prepared. They were not financially able to sustain the lifestyle and had thought they would be able to anchor most of the time. The weather, however, is not always conducive to this and, as in this couple's case, they realised they would have to pay heavy mooring fees at marinas in order to survive.

We left them next morning with advice about the weather and their route. They would journey back to the UK, abandoning their dream of sailing to the Caribbean.

Talking of the Caribbean, our next stop, San José, was very much like the Caribbean. In the 80's, it was a small marina with a few motorboats and yachts moored near to the most beautiful tropical-looking beach with palm trees dotted everywhere. We have since visited Barbados several times and remember that San José was very similar to some of the beaches there. The voyage from Garrucha was uneventful, and we were delighted to see that San José was in stark contrast - seemingly a tropical paradise. Apart from being awakened in the night by noisy teenagers holding parties on peoples' motorboats, we were content to stay there for two nights enjoying swimming in the warm sea, eating in delightful merenderos (picnic areas) on the beach, and watching television in the clubhouse.

This year's journey was nearing its close and I was interested to see the Cabo de Gata headland where the honeymooners at Garrucha had spent a miserable week sheltering from the wind.

I had a personal interest in the area since my grandfather, Clarence Louis Oldfield, had sailed on a ship named Glenorchy in the area in the 1900's. The ship sank just off Cabo de Gata headland in a collision with SS Atlantide on a voyage from Chile to Massiglia in 1915. Built in 1882, Glenorchy was an iron ship originally rigged with royal sails over double top and single topgallant sails; she was later re-rigged as a four-masted barque. I thought about my grandfather as we sailed in moderate winds past the distinctive headland, bound for Almería.

We intended to visit the Cabo de Gata-Níjar Natural Park, a reserve near Almería characterised by volcanic rock formations. The area is semiarid and the driest location in Europe. We made a mental note to visit this unique and unspoiled area when we had finally settled into Almerimar marina.

Winds of force 4 - 5 took us swiftly towards the port city of Almería (on the Costa de Almería). We entered the huge harbour, not sure whether to tie up against the town wall or to anchor. We finally decided to tie up; dwarfed by the high seawall and large vessels next to us. We had not been there very long when the Guardia Civil came along looking smart in their uniforms - also somewhat threatening with guns in their holsters. We were used to their visits by now, as they had come aboard the yacht in most harbours, they thus had a record of our comings and goings since we had first entered Spain via the Gulf of Lion.

This time though we were surprised to find that they sat and chatted with us, smoking cigarettes whilst checking our passports. That was until we noticed a formidable looking police officer, seemingly of high rank, shouting to them from the quay. They were obviously trying to avoid him and thought they would come aboard our yacht for a break and a smoke, but had not got away with it. We laughed with them as they climbed up the town quay steps to face the wrath of the officer.

An English couple by the name of John and Margaret in a *Westerley* yacht were anchored in the centre of the harbour and rowed over in their dinghy to ask us aboard for drinks. We were to form a friendship with them for the rest of our time in Spain that year.

Despite the difficulty in climbing up and down the town wall, we took time the next day to discover Almería and visited the Alcazaba, the second largest Moorish castle amongst the Muslim fortresses of Andalucía after the Alhambra in Granada.

We also went in search of a nice beach to have a swim. "Not another nudist beach!" we cried when we found we were on the largest naturist beach in Europe, surrounded by naturist accommodation. We decided against swimming, as the people frying in the sun were not a pretty sight.

Instead of swimming and lying on the beach, we took a bus to explore the surrounding countryside and were amazed to see miles of plastic tents covering the arid landscape. We realised that Almería's economy was based on agriculture; the plastic tents were green houses that produce tons of fruit and vegetables with more than 70% being exported to the rest of Europe.

We could understand why the numerous spaghetti western films were made in the region of Almería, as the terrain was very desert-like and arid. In the 80's, there was a placed called 'Hollywood' which was attracting tourists in large numbers - possibly in the hope of catching a glimpse of Clint Eastwood? Some of the film sets still exist.

The bus ride was an adventure in itself, with Flamenco music blaring out and local people shouting to one another above the music. Spanish people, we found, love noise and it doesn't bother them - the noisier, the better. In most countries, it would not be allowed for the bus driver to hold conversations with the passengers, but there was a constant stream of passengers standing beside him whilst he was driving - holding loud conversations, and more worryingly, the driver was gesticulating wildly whilst turning dangerous corners.

We breathed a sigh of relief when we arrived back safely at Almería bus station as we were beginning to wonder whether we would arrive back at the yacht in one piece.

Our friends, John and Margaret, had braved the nudists and were returning from the beach looking rather sunburned. We told them we were leaving for Almerimar next morning and they said they would follow on later and meet up there.

We motored out of Almería harbour, passing some huge craft on the way and being caught up in the wash, but fortunately, the sea was moderate as soon as we were clear. We put up the mainsail and the jib and looked forward to this, the final leg of our journey, before returning to the UK for the winter months.

We remembered the tip from the pilot book and the couple at Mar Menor: we were to look out for three imposing high-rise blocks of apartments that were situated at the eastern most point of the marina. Once we had spotted these, we could apparently then proceed towards the dique and the entrance.

The wind, of course, was in the wrong direction, so eventually we had to take the mainsail down, and proceeded under engine and jib. As we neared the block of apartments, the weather started to take a turn for the worse and a savage squall blew up - it wasn't even time for the *Afternoon Hate*. We battled on with the spray in our face and *Ipi'n tombia* leaping about in the heightening waves. At last, Brian spotted the dique through his binoculars and without further ado, we took down the jib and motored towards the entrance.

The approach was impressive; a modern building in the shape of a tower stood to our port as we motored in. Two mariners stood on the quay and shouted to us, but the wind was so strong, we couldn't hear what they were trying to say. We continued to motor on. We then spotted them again, this time

121

on mopeds waving frantically, so we followed their directions. The marina was the best we'd ever seen, but quiet, with only a few very luxurious motorboats and luxury yachts moored near the tower. On our right as we sailed into the visitors' area of the marina, we spotted a restaurant, Club Nautique with people sitting out on chairs, waving to us. There were a few shops and apartments surrounding the area and we were directed to moor in a corner at the end of the quay opposite some shops. The wind was buffeting us about a lot and we were very grateful for the mariners' assistance as we tied up and made the yacht secure.

Before we could take stock, though, the mariners insisted we went to the tower (which turned out to be the Capitán's office) to show our passports and book our yacht into the marina.

This we did, and when we told the affable young Spanish man sitting behind a huge desk that we would like to book our yacht in for a year, he was very impressed and we proceeded to negotiate a price with him. The new marina had berths for 1,000 yachts but was practically empty apart from a few of the larger luxury yachts and so we were able to strike a bargain and get a good price.

He told us that the marina was in the process of being completed and the whole area was going to be a pleasure area for holidaymakers, with golf courses, swimming pools, tennis and every facility for the yachtsman, rather like Empuriabrava we thought.

The nearest supermarket was run by a Spanish man who spoke good English. Coincidentally, he had lived in Newport, South Wales, during the period we lived nearby at Chepstow, Monmouthshire. The supermarket was the only one in the area at the time and was situated in what was called the Commercial Centre where entertainment took place such as Spanish dancing at weekends.

It was quite a long walk to the supermarket from our yacht, but we took our faithful trolley with us and trekked through bush land where stray dogs roamed at night but disappeared during the day.

The shop was crammed full with every type of food. A surly Spanish butcher served us with some meat for our barbecue. His shop was situated up some stairs at the top of the grocery section, whilst downstairs was a fresh fish section with the catch of the day prominently displayed.

It was so nice to be settled in one place, not having to prepare to set off again the next day. We cleaned the yacht from top to bottom and decided to stay put for a couple of weeks before we booked our flights to return to the UK to see what our children had been up to in our absence.

The nearest town was El Ejido - a working town consisting of one main street with shops branching off it. We asked where the nearest bus stop was and were told by some English holidaymakers that they had waited for over an hour for one that had not turned up - they told us not to be surprised if we had the same problem.

They were right, the one we thought we were going to catch turned up half an hour late, but this was Spain, and we were relaxed. After all, we had all the time on our hands and each day was another adventure, never knowing what was going to happen next.

We found the Banco de Andalucía on the main street in El Ejido and drew some money ready to pay for our airfares home. We also noticed a travel agency just opposite, and went in to enquire about flights. We booked up to return two weeks later. After being immersed in the culture of Spain for so long, it was a strange feeling to think about flying and going back to a very different lifestyle.

We then sat out on the pavement outside a delightful little café, ordered dos café con leche, and watched the various local characters go by.

Afterwards, we wandered into the pretty market square where there was a vegetable and flower market. Satisfied with our leisurely explorations in the town, we found a bus stop and sat down on a bench waiting hopefully for a bus to take us back to the marina, El Puerto Deportivo de Almerimar.

Opposite us was a bench that seated just two people and we noticed a Spanish man sitting there. His wife turned up looking as though she was in the last days of pregnancy and carrying huge shopping bags. His friend, another Spanish man, appeared about the same time and he gestured for him to sit down, leaving his wife to stand for about quarter of an hour whilst a heated conversation between all three of them took place. Spanish men were very macho in the 80's; not so many Spanish women went out to work, but kept house and cared for their children.

The bus eventually turned up and the pregnant woman was left to struggle onto the bus with all her bags whilst the two men carried on with their conversation on the bench. We did our best to help her find a seat for which she was very grateful and thanked us.

Each balmy day ran into another. We rose at 7am, walked to the beach for a swim in the deserted bay, and enjoyed the occasional day sail to keep our hand in. We were really enjoying our last days in Spain until Brian woke up one night with terrible toothache, and then one of his teeth broke off.

We enquired in the Capitán's office where we could find a dentist and they told us we had to go to El Ejido. The bus miraculously turned up on time and we had been told the dentist was near to the Banco de Andalucía so we knew where to go. Brian went in by himself whilst I waited for him nearby, enjoying a café con leche.

He reappeared looking rather bemused after about an hour and told me that the dentist couldn't speak a word of English - he hoped he had taken the right tooth out. He wasn't sure he was in the right place, since halfway through the proceedings, the dentist rushed to the room next door where a woman was in labour - he attended to her and then came back to Brian. This happened about three times until Brian heard the sound of a baby crying, so in between taking Brian's tooth out, he had also delivered a baby.

This is what we loved about Spain. Everything was so relaxed and laid back - you never knew what to expect next.

The morning we left for England, we felt sad to leave *Ipi 'n tombia*. She had served us so well on our adventure from England to Southern Spain.

Almería Airport was a modest and pretty airport. We sat at a table surrounded by colourful flowers in pots outside a restaurant and enjoying a cool drink whilst we waited for our plane to arrive.

A shock, however, was to await us when we arrived back at our house on Canvey Island, and one we had never anticipated.

Chapter 16

Our house had been rented to a fairly well known pop group consisting of four musicians, so we were prepared for the worst when we arrived home after being so long away.

We had expected the house to be in ruins and the neighbours complaining, but were surprised to see that the house had been left in immaculate condition. Even the curtains and carpets had been cleaned and not a thing out of place. The garden had been well tended and none of this was due to the care of the estate agent; the boys in the group had hired a housekeeper and a gardener.

We did get a minor complaint from our next-door neighbours who said they did tend to practice their music quite a bit, but as they were such nice boys, they forgave them.

This was a relief and we set about becoming landlubbers once again - preparing for a cold winter as it was now October and already we were finding it difficult to adapt to grey skies.

After a good night's sleep in a comfortable bed for a change, we were having breakfast when the phone rang and I picked it up. A panicky voice came on the other end of the line and it took me some time to realise it was the wife of the client we had sold the house and warehouse to in Salou.

"I thought I should phone you," she said. "I've only just arrived back in England from Spain and have been in prison there for three months."

I wondered what she was talking about and asked her to clarify what she meant. Apparently, her husband - unbeknown to her - had used the warehouse he bought to store drugs behind the tiles on the wall. He had been caught red handed. Unfortunately, she was there at the time and had been sentenced to prison for a couple of months. Although she had now been released, her husband was still in prison.

Evidently, he had been smuggling drugs for some time. It dawned on us that this was what he was using his motorboat for when travelling between Gibraltar and Morocco on a regular basis.

We discovered that the police had been tracking him for many months and had followed him to Spain where he was arrested. We were thankful that we were not implicated in any way, as he had been referred to us by the estate agent in Kent - he had not come directly to us to purchase the property. We were also grateful that our trip from France through to Spain was recorded by the authorities, and the Guardia Civil had kept details of our movements right the way through to Almerimar.

I felt very sorry for the woman, as her husband had kept her completely in the dark about his devious activities in the drug smuggling world.

After a grey winter in England, we made plans to set out once to Almerimar and continue our journey down the coast to the Costa del Sol (Coast of the Sun).

On a summer morning, we set out for Gatwick Airport complete with luggage to last us for a few months as we planned to spend the entire summer cruising.

It was a great feeling to be back in Spain and heading for our life at sea, away from the humdrum greyness of the British winter, and equally grey faces of the people as they went about their daily business.

The yacht looked good in her new mooring but the decks needing scrubbing badly, and that was the first task we undertook once we were aboard and had enjoyed a cool drink. We noticed a yacht in very good condition next to us belonging to a friendly German man, Jochen, who would became our best friend whilst we were in Almerimar and remains so to this day.

We informed the Capitán's office that we would be away for several months, but would be returning to Almerimar after our extended cruise. We motored out of the marina after topping up with 40 litres of diesel heading for the port of Adra, a few miles west of Almerimar. We were keen try out a new toy we had brought with us from England - an autopilot. The wind was light from the west and it was wonderful to be out at sea again.

We soon spotted the small commercial fishing port of Adra and dropped anchor in the middle of the harbour. There were no other yachts anywhere to be seen and just two or three fishing boats tied against the harbour wall, so it was a very peaceful setting.

We stayed just the one night in Adra, as we were keen to move on further up the coast. At 8am, we started the engine and called to a passing fisherman who was heading out to sea in his boat. We enquired about the weather and he replied that it would be a Levante wind (blowing from the east) but less than force 6, so we considered it would be okay to proceed.

When we got out to sea, however, we realised that the fisherman should have told us it was blowing force 6 - and above!

We kept the engine running, as the sea was decidedly choppy, with just half the genoa (large jib) up and no mainsail. As we neared Cabo Sacratif, the seas became huge and it was like being in the Gulf of Lion again - only rougher, as the waves were breaking into the cockpit and I got soaked sitting at the tiller. I was trying to head in the direction of the next port, Motril, a town and municipality in the province of Granada.

After a hair-raising couple of hours, we finally spotted the dique and headed for the marina, but it was so rough that we couldn't see any empty moorings, so we made for the town quay where several fishing boats were tied up. We had just managed to tie onto a bollard when a mariner approached us and told us we couldn't tie up there, which we thought was rather unfair of him, as the weather was appalling. We could hardly hear what he was saying, but he pointed to the marina. Our attempt to inform him that there were no free berths in the marina was in vain; he ignored us, untied our warps and sent us back out into the harbour. Here, we finally managed to drop anchor, which we thought was a miraculous achievement as we were being buffeted about by both wind and waves.

By the time we had made the anchor fast with another warp, the wind was gusting to gale force 8.

A very bumpy night followed, with hardly any sleep, so when we rose next morning, we were glad to see that the storm had abated and the sea was calm - enough to allow us to drop the *Bombard* dinghy over the side. We motored towards the marina in order to look for supplies in the town of Motril.

As soon as we went to tie up the dinghy, however, a formidable looking Spaniard appeared dressed in a blazer and told us we were not allowed ashore. His manner was very condescending and we hadn't realised at the time, but he must have assumed we were anchoring in the harbour, as we couldn't afford to moor in the marina. He overlooked perhaps, that there were no berths available, and that we had arrived in the middle of a bad storm.

We ignored him, headed back to the yacht, and set out for our next destination. The weather was much improved and, because of our bad experience in Motril, we were glad to leave - making a mental note not to call in at that marina again unless we were forced to.

I had particularly wanted to stop at Almuñecar, a town situated between the village of Nerja and Motril in the subtropical area of coastline known as the Costa Tropical. I had read of its history and that since the death of Francisco Franco in 1975, the town had become the most important tourist town in Granada. Also, it is an important setting in Laurie Lee's account of the outbreak of the Spanish Civil War in his book *As I Walked Out One Midsummer Morning*.

We decided, however, to pass by the town and instead drop anchor between two headlands further along the coast at La Herradura. The weather was reasonably calm when we arrived, so we lowered the dinghy and rowed ashore, buying ice creams on the beach and spending a lazy afternoon sunbathing. It was not a good choice of anchoring, though; the wind blew up in the night and we were thrown all over the place. It was also too rough to raise anchor and head towards the shelter on the lee of the headland.

Our plan to stay a couple of nights in this anchorage went out of the window and so we set off in calmer seas; the wind had died down, there was only a gentle ripple on the water and hardly enough wind to fill the sails.

Although rough sailing in windy weather can be very exhilarating, it can also be frightening. Concentration is vital, as one wrong move and the yacht can broach violently or pitch into a wave, but I had great faith in Brian - my husband and skipper. We worked well together in all weathers, and the more sailing we did, the more experience we gained, and the better and stronger we became.

The trip to Marina del Este, our next port of call, was relaxed and enjoyable. The sun was shining and the sea was calm, so we enjoyed having our lunch in the cockpit and taking it in turns to look out for the next dique. Our automatic pilot had proved to be invaluable; calibrated and set correctly, it guided us to wherever we wanted to go.

The entrance to the beautiful Marina del Este was very difficult to find. Large cliffs blocked the view until the very last moment when we had to make a sharp turn towards the entrance. It would be easy to miss it altogether.

We'd heard that the marina had been closed because of rockslides due to considerable building taking place by developers constructing holiday villas on the side of the steep hill. We looked out for a chain that would block the entrance if the marina were closed - in which case we would have moved on to the next marina.

We were lucky, however, and astonished at how pretty the marina was. A mariner helped us tie up at a convenient mooring near to some shops surrounding the quay. We checked in at the Capitán's office for two nights. Unlike many marinas that were either too big or touristy, or without any facilities at all, this marina appeared to have been built with the yachtsman's interests at heart. There were showers and toilet facilities, diesel, water available, and not only grocery shops - clothing stores with the latest fashions and delightful restaurants and cafés.

The fees were not cheap, but despite this, some luxurious boats of all shapes and sizes were moored permanently there.

The only disadvantage was perhaps the marina's proximity. To get to the nearest town or even the main road, you had to take a hire car or taxi to negotiate a long steep hill. The marina was very self-contained to meet the requirements of the boating fraternity, so it was a case of using local services or spending time and money to travel further afield.

Still, it was such a pretty setting, we felt no need to go exploring this time, and enjoyed our two days' rest before setting out for our next destination where we would spend the rest of the summer months.

Chapter 17

Caleta de Vélez. We sailed into the Spanish fishing port of Caleta de Vélez unaware of how fascinating and colourful our stay would be. In the early 90's, the town was still very Spanish and steeped in the old traditional ways. The port was primarily for fishermen whose livelihood depended on the catch of the day; the fish was prepared in the processing plant on the quay and sold to local women who came with their shopping baskets to bargain with the fishermen.

The village is situated on the coastline approximately thirty kilometres east of Málaga on the Costa del Sol. Once isolated from big towns, it maintained a self-sufficiency, with shops, bars and cafés situated along the roadside amidst modest whitewashed houses where families and elderly people mixed and lived in close harmony.

The shops bars and cafés were mainly frequented by the Spanish population and tourists were hardly in evidence - apart from the occasional visiting yachtsman stopping at the fishing port on the way to Gibraltar or further afield.

There was a semblance of a marina for visiting yachts and motorboats, but it was only half completed. When we arrived, we managed to throw our warps to a passing fisherman who tied us on to the quay and told us there was an office nearby where we could check whether we could stay for any length of time.

We looked around for water and diesel but none was to be found, so we were not certain how long we could stay with supplies. We got talking to a Spaniard who spoke fluent English and lived permanently on a large rather neglected boat at the end of the quay. He told us we could get water from the town square, if we carried our water can with us, and diesel from a nearby garage. We were used to doing this in our trip down the coast from France so didn't find it a hardship at all.

In fact, we began to enjoy our daily trek to the fountain in the town square; here we met many interesting characters also collecting water, as many of the houses didn't have a water supply.

Spanish gypsies were frequent visitors to the fountain. Amongst them were some colourful characters: large sunburned mothers with brown naked babies chewing on pieces of bread, dark, interesting men with flashing eyes and lean bodies, wearing sombreros jauntily on the side of their heads. We found that many of the gypsies earned their living by fishing and selling their catch on the side of the road to the villagers.

Regularly, we saw them pushing old bicycles along the road, shouting *pescado* (fish) at the top of their voices. The Spanish ladies, many dressed in black even in the hottest of weather, would stroll up to them and start to argue about the price of fish. Many of the older generation of Spanish women traditionally wore black when any member of their family died, no matter how close a relative they were; it could have been a long removed second cousin. At the time of our visit, however, the custom was beginning to die out.

Washing clothes on a yacht is a problem when you have very limited water, but I found a primitive place where the local gypsy women did their washing. It was located near to the village fountain where there was also a tap for rinsing, so I watched with interest and saw them beating their washing unmercifully against two stone basins with their children clinging to their legs.

The housing for many of the gypsies was also primitive - tiny houses positioned along the main street, where at night we could look in through the open doorways. One such house had an overstuffed armchair outside the door and poor furnishings inside, but like all Spanish peoples' accommodation, it was spotlessly clean. We often stopped to give the children some spare pesetas for which the gypsy mothers always seemed very grateful.

The weather by now was very hot and we found that it was the custom of Spanish families to visit the beach on

Sundays. Those who had cars or vans would load up with tents, umbrellas, barbecues and set them all up on the beach ready to spend the day there.

Caleta de Vélez was situated between two towns, namely Torre del Mar and Torrox. These towns were gradually turning into tourist areas because of the long stretch of beach. We would often walk to the beaches, have a swim, and take a much-needed shower, as these were freely available on the beach. We also discovered a lavandería (laundry) in Torre del Mar, so occasionally - when I didn't join the gypsies in the town square - I used to take all our bedding and clothes.

My Spanish was by now fairly good and I found myself having conversations with all sorts of Spanish people, including the gypsies. They were always very appreciative that I had made the effort to speak to them in their language. We had many invitations to join in their activities, including teenagers' parties on the beach, which were a bit hair-raising, as they kept disappearing behind the rocks to get up to goodness knows what. We went to Spanish dancing events in the local hall and were impressed by the shows - much different to the tourist shows, that in no way match the authentic Spanish gypsy dancing we experienced.

We particularly loved the evenings sitting in the cockpit on the yacht watching the sun go down behind the mountains, leaving a kaleidoscope of magnificent colour in its wake. This is when the Spanish villagers came alive. They would dress themselves and their children in their best finery, take a stroll (paseo) through the fishing port, and looking at all the boats. When they spotted that we were on board, they spoke and laughed with us.

Chairs would be put outside the houses on the pavements and whole families would sit outside in the cool of the evening with children running around the feet of their parents and grandchildren.

On such an evening, we took a stroll through the village and noticed a very old oxen cart made out of wood with two huge wooden wheels and yokes for two oxen. We were fascinated by the cart, stopped to have a look, and noticed a little door at the side of a house standing wide open. Noticing our interest a Spanish gentleman came through the door; we asked him what the cart was for and with that, he invited us into a cool low ceiling room. It was like the room of a small house, but instead, housed two oxen together with their calves that were munching hay from loose boxes. It struck us how clean the room was, with no odour at all, and next door was the family living quarters.

The Spanish man told us that they were part of his family - during the day they worked in the sugarcane fields nearby and his family had been in the sugar business for many years.

This family was typical of the friendly people to be found in the old Spanish pueblos and towns along the coast. We often sat on deck at night in the fishing port, hearing the jingle of the oxens' bells as they plodded their way happily from the sugarcane fields.

We decided to visit Nerja on the bus - a town I was very familiar with, as over the years, I had worked there on a regular basis. It was still a pretty town, but in the 80's when I first went there, it was just a small fishing village. Now, however, it was emerging into yet another tourist area, which I felt quite upset about - I had a soft spot for Nerja.

We had no idea where to catch the bus and so we asked in three different shops - the fish shop (pescadería), the bakery, and finally the butchers. All recommended different places and different times, but we finally decided to take the word of a woman called Gloria at the butchers. She said the bus stop was right outside her shop door, and we did indeed notice a glass case with a timetable inside so, yes, this must be the bus stop?

The next morning, we gave ourselves plenty of time, arriving at 9am, but to our dismay there was no sign of the glass case with the timetable. Also, no sign of Gloria, and no sign of anyone else waiting.

There was a bench on the side of the pavement, however, so we sat down hoping that a bus would finally appear. Half an hour later, a Spanish gypsy lady appeared with her young son who was misbehaving - she was shouting loudly at him. We were amused to see she had a bag on her shoulder on which was written in large pink letters, "Kiss me Stupid" in English. We were certain she had no idea what it meant and had probably just picked the bag up as a bargain at the local market.

I asked her if she was waiting for the bus, and whether it would be going to Nerja. She replied that she going there, so eventually we all piled onto the bus - which was already full of people - and hoped the driver wouldn't take the hairpin bends at top speed as most bus drivers did in Spain.

Chapter 18

Fiesta time in Caleta de Vélez in honour of the Virgen del Carmen is a magnificent four-day carnival of colour, action and beauty, with the local fishing families throwing themselves whole-heartedly into all the proceedings. It took place in July when we were there - the hottest time of the year when no one goes to bed before 2am.

We had lived amongst the Spanish people in Caleta for a month, had begun to appreciate their simple way of life, and were beginning to know the characters of these warm, friendly people.

A few days before the fiesta, one can sense the anticipation amongst the fishing families, particularly the children. It is one of the biggest celebrations of the year, and as most of the Spanish people are devout Roman Catholics, a very important religious event.

The start was heralded by the local marathon, when all the local sports people limbered up at the start line dressed in a devastating array of colourful sports gear. The starter gun fired and they leapt away amidst the shouting and cheering of the crowds of people on the pavement, who spent the rest of the morning rushing round to strategic points to catch a glimpse of the runners as they raced through the streets, their bodies perspiring in the hot July sun.

Football followed in the afternoon, and when the weary players finished their game and returned home to a cool shower, they afterwards danced the night away at the disco situated in the fairground. Then, a dramatic display of flamenco dancing ensued, whilst outside, fireworks cascaded like a thousand tiny stars out to sea, *oohs* and *aahs* resounding in the hot night air.

Caleta de Vélez was alive with festivity for three hectic days leading up to the majestic procession of the Virgen del Carmen, which was to take place on the fourth and final day.

The statue of the Virgen del Carmen is housed in the local church (or *The Casa* as the Spanish fishermen say). Once a year, on the 16th July, she is carried from the church by Spanish bearers dressed in black trousers, red cummerbunds, and short-sleeved white shirts.

The Virgen was preceded by a large band of marching school children dressed in smart uniforms moving slowly and rhythmically to the heavy beat of the drum that set the pace for the slow procession. The local villagers of all ages, jostled for a place on the crowded pavements, and balconies on the houses overlooking the street were packed with people.

Luckily, Brian and I had secured a good place in the crowds to watch. The statue of the Virgen emerged - seated on a plinth surrounded by beautiful flowers, carrying her small baby, her face translucent and ethereal in the glow of flickering candles that surrounded her. She moved majestically from the church along the crowded streets towards the fishing port.

Police were directing traffic away from the procession, whistling loudly at errant motorists trying to sneak their way through the crowds.

We could feel the crowd's anticipation and awe as the mystical spectacle drew closer. Pretty Spanish girls in colourful traditional dresses, and small boys in toreador outfits wearing jaunty Spanish hats, caught their breath as they gazed in wonder at the grace and beauty of their idol moving slowly past them.

On the tiny terraces of the houses on either side of the street, families added to the colour and excitement, holding brightly coloured torches in honour of the Virgen del Carmen as she passed by, their faces rapt as they gazed at the spectacle. They were families of the fishing fleet and held the belief that the Virgen protects their men folk from harm when they at sea. The faith and trust they felt was evident in their eyes as she passed.

The procession came to a halt just outside the gates of the fishing port and the children posed for photographs in front of the statue. The crowds on the quay surged forward to catch a glimpse. Slowly, gently swaying, the procession moved forward towards the fleet - fifty fishing boats proudly waiting in the harbour, their many flags fluttering in welcome to the much-revered Virgen del Carmen.

They waited whilst she was slowly, reverently, moved to the place of honour on the largest boat of the fishing fleet, resplendent with flags, bunting, and flowers. Spanish fishing families and tourists mingled on the quay to watch as the Virgen awaited her journey on the boat out to sea.

Crowds lined the sea walls and cheered as the numerous fishing boats surged forward at some speed in the still hot evening - the moon casting an eerie glow on the procession rushing out to sea. Excitement gathered as the fifty fishing boats vied for position, fanning out in all directions along the coast, their powerful engines racing. The spectators roared in delight as momentum gathered and many tiny motorboats joined the melee. Their spray spilled around them, bursting into a cascade of sparkling phosphorescence as they jostled their way through the waves, trying to catch up with the fishing boats. Fishermen in their brightly lit boats cast their fishing lamps on the magnificent scene, giving added illumination to the splendour for all to see. Cheering from the crowds on the quay blended with the chanting aboard the boats.

The Virgen del Carmen sat majestically in her place of honour with her child clutched to her breast on the master 'ship', her proud face in profile against the flickering of the many candles surrounding her throne tended by the bearers. Her ship joined the turmoil of racing fishing boats whose main objective appeared to be to get as close as possible to her.

The fishing boats, to the delight of the crowds, converged at great speed on the master ship chanting, "Long live beautiful lady!" They raced alongside the brightly lit ship, each one trying to catch one more glimpse of the Virgen.

Noise from the crowds and the fishing boats reached a crescendo, until reluctantly, one by one, the fishing boats turned back towards the port - crowding ever closer to the master ship to catch a glimpse of the Virgen del Carmen as she pulled alongside the quay.

Tumultuous crowds greeted her, and it was some time before the bearers were able to raise the plinth on to their broad shoulders in readiness for the gentle swaying walk along the quay back to *The Casa*. The band of schoolchildren assembled in front of her and played bugles in time with the heavy beat of the drum as they swayed towards the gates leading into the village of Caleta de Vélez.

Here, the bearers gently placed the Virgen down in readiness for a spectacular fireworks display in her honour. The fireworks cascaded above the sea whilst the crowds gasped in awe and wonder at the spectacular sight - still reluctant to take their eyes off the Virgen del Carmen.

Finally, the bearers raised the heavy plinth on to their shoulders and resumed the slow swaying walk back to *The Casa* where the Virgen del Carmen would repose until the following year when the men of the sea would honour her again.

This was one of the most moving fiestas Brian and I had witnessed during our journey through France and Spain; perhaps a fitting finale to this part of a wonderful journey, and a lifestyle that was to continue for many years to come.

But do not hurry the journey at all
Better that it should last many years
Be quite old when you anchor at the island
Rich with all you have gained on the way

Extract: 'Ithaca' by Constantine P. Cavafy

Visit the author website with more details of
books by Eugenie C Smith at
http://eugeniecsmithbooks.wordpress.com/